Everyday Creative is a must read for any⟨ work yet struggles to liberate their creati about his readers, translating the energy and excitement he generates on stages the world over into an infectious and inspiring read.

Layne Beachley AO, 7-Time World Champion Surfer.

Modern Magician, enlightened speaker, solar human being, Mykel Dixon is translating his subtle and extraordinary work in this much needed recovery book. With a bit of fear and hopefully great excitement, dive into this guide to find again the amazing, creative, powerful human being in you. A must read for any leader in this time of deep change!

Eglantine Etiemble, Executive General Manager Digital, DuluxGroup

Everyday Creative is brazenly heretical; a poetic affront to the business world—which is *exactly* what we need right now. Like a best-friend-in-a-book, you'll (re)discover how to tap into the creativity and courage you've always had. Everyone needs this book—buy it for your bedside, bathroom and boardroom!

Dr Jason Fox, wizard and best-selling author of
How to Lead a Quest

Creativity is the defining currency of the 21st century. This book doesn't just make a compelling case for embracing a more creative approach at work, it shows you how. An instant classic written by a guy who lives and breathes his message.

Jules Lund, founder, Tribe

Mykel has the unique ability to speak to both head and heart as he challenges us to bring our full creative potential to life. This book is a challenging, heart-warming, soul-searching read that help you excavate your unique flair and fulfil your creative destiny. Read if you dare!

Dean Summlar, Vice President Human Resources - Pacific Zone, Schneider Electric

Everyday Creative should be mandatory reading for executives who want to not only stay ahead of the curve but help redefine what a curve is. A stirring read from an entrepreneur who has walked the walk, time and time again.

David Swan, Technology Editor, *The Australian*

EVERY DAY CREATIVE

MYKEL DIXON

EVERY

A DANGEROUS GUIDE

DAY

TO MAKING

CREA

MAGIC AT WORK

TIVE

WILEY

First published in 2020 by John Wiley & Sons Australia, Ltd
42 McDougall St, Milton Qld 4064

Office also in Melbourne

Typeset in ITC Stone Serif Std 9/14pt

ISBN: 978-0-730-38373-4

A catalogue record for this book is available from the National Library of Australia

Cover design and 'Mykes' images: © Oli Sansom

Internal images: © JungleOutThere/iStockphoto; © Ye Liew/Shutterstock; © 4x6/iStockphoto; © KeithBishop/Getty Images

10 9 8 7 6 5 4 3 2 1

Disclaimer

Table of Contents

Part Two
Developing The Practice | 73

Part Three
Making Your Masterpiece | 167

About Mykel

Mykel Dixon is mad about shaking up the way we do business.

A musician by trade, gypsy by nature, fierce non-conformist and prolific anti-perfectionist, he leads a new wave of entrepreneurial savants showing forward-thinking companies how to stay relevant and radical in a 21st-Century Renaissance.

As an award-winning speaker, learning designer, event curator, musician and author, Mykel works with senior leaders and teams of Fortune 500 and ASX 200 companies to unlock breakthrough creativity. His clients include Google, YouTube, Janssen, Schneider Electric, Intuit, Bayer, IAG, CBA, Telstra, Origin, Lululemon, Laminex and Seek, amongst many others.

Mykel's unconventional life (and career) experience, coupled with his daring vision for the future of work, make him the not-so-secret weapon for any company seeking an edge.

To find out more about Myke, enquire about speaking opportunities and follow his creative adventures online, head to www.mykeldixon.com

A Story

Given the state of world I questioned whether I should even write this book. Surely there are better ways for me to have a meaningful impact on the world? Maybe I'd do more for humanity by chaining myself to a tree, becoming a firefighter, or going into politics (yuk!). Surely the world doesn't need another bloody book, least of all one by me.

But I couldn't shake the idea. When I look at the world around us, and the challenges we now face as individuals and teams, as companies and nations — it seems like the only thing that will make a meaningful difference is our ability to think and act *differently*. To have the courage to think beyond what's achievable, to dream beyond what's reasonable, and build products, services and experiences that go beyond what is merely profitable.

In my current work as a keynote speaker, creative facilitator and experience designer, I am privileged to meet people from all walks of life. I get paid to engage in deep conversations about work, career and success. About the past, present and future. About money, meaning and magic. And what underpins it all is creativity.

Through all the wild activations and immersive experiences that I design and deliver, the answer to so many of the challenges that people speak about is the same. Creativity.

Time and time again I see the same thing: people who wholeheartedly believe they aren't creative find a way back to their natural self-expression, then apply it in their work to cultivate staggering positive results.

I see people walk into the room tired, frustrated and complacent only to leave vibrant, energised and enthusiastic. People who have 'seen it all before' end up staying longer than they had planned. People who 'don't have much to say' end up sharing more than they intended. People who are known for being serious end up laughing louder than they've laughed in months (sometimes years).

Creativity is the catalyst for professional success and personal fulfilment.

When I reflect on my own life, the one characteristic that has served me most, hands down, is creativity. It's been the source of my security, satisfaction and sense of self. The essence of my competitive advantage and the instrument that led to any and all of my career success.

I began my career as a musician. From jazz to rock, covers to originals, empty hotel lobbies to main stages of music festivals—creativity was my currency. And yet beyond the obvious application of creativity in my songwriting or performances, it was in fact the key driver of every element of my business.

From sales and marketing to PR and event production. From conflict resolution to crisis management. It enabled me to think differently about every challenge or opportunity and respond in ways that were unique, distinct and original. It was, without a doubt, my secret weapon.

Like so many professional artists, at various points in my career I also flirted with casual jobs to supplement my income. I've been a nanny, a barista, a security guard, an industrial cleaner, a beach bar owner, a website builder, a copywriter, a call-centre operator and a community manager, to name a few.

And every slice of success or fulfilment that I experienced in each of those jobs was the direct result of creativity. Perhaps I had to be creative to get the position or to outperform my peers. To navigate the unknown or build meaningful (and profitable) relationships. To stand out or fit in. To lead the charge or toe the line.

Without creativity I'd be nothing, nowhere and no-one.

It's through my own direct experience that I've come to believe creativity is the number one driver of personal fulfilment and professional success. And that its value in the emerging economic climate is accelerating every day.

Which is how we ended up here, having this conversation at this time. This book is my attempt to share what I've learned so that you might find a little of the same joy and opportunity that I have, while making the world a bit more magical and beautiful along the way.

Enjoy.

Introduction

Over the last few years, I've asked hundreds of people to describe what comes to mind when they first hear the word 'creativity'. The following are a small collection of real responses:

≈ endless possibility, borderless thinking, joyful expression

≈ fun, freedom, playfulness, curiosity, energy, excitement, colour, vibrancy, authenticity, vulnerability, uniqueness, originality

≈ letting go of control, hands in the air, challenging the norm, thinking outside the box, living life on your own terms, making yourself and others smile.

I then ask them to describe *their* relationship to creativity. Here are some of the responses:

≈ love/hate, long-distance, frayed, tortured

≈ 'It's something I love but don't prioritise enough in both work and life'; stigma around it being frivolous, indulgent and a waste of time

≈ 'I crave the time to dream up new solutions and play with interesting ideas but almost always suppress it because of the constant pressure to deliver.'

≈ 'It's something I know I have but often squander to get the job done. And whenever I do that I'm never satisfied with the result.'

≈ 'It's the thing that brings me the most joy but also the thing I find most difficult to dedicate time to.'

And when I ask them to define their *company's* relationship to creativity, I hear this:

≈ nonexistent, complicated, misunderstood, delusional

≈ 'There's a desire for more creativity but it's mostly suffocated by process and bureaucracy.'

≈ 'It's encouraged, especially on training days, but it often gets lost in the day-to-day pressure to get results.'

≈ 'There's an openness to it and a recognition that the traditional path won't get us where we need to go. However, there is a dominant, well-established operating model supported by people at all levels of the organisation who primarily value safety and certainty.'

So here we see the dysfunctional love triangle that exists between creativity, business and us.

We love it, we value it and we want more of it in our work and life. But we can't seem to squeeze it into our overflowing task list. And despite our company calling for more innovative thinking, the systems and processes that hold the business together don't seem to enable it.

This book sets out to solve this sticky situation. To give you simple tools to recover your innate creativity (if you feel you've lost it) or amplify it in your work and life (if it's just a little blocked). To reaffirm for you that creativity is the foundation of finding and forming new value, which makes it the strongest driver of your competitive advantage and commercial success.

By the time we finish our conversation, it is my hope that you become more than just an Everyday Creative, but a loud, vocal advocate for its value in life and *especially at work*.

Defining Everyday Creativity

To try and define creativity is like trying to hold smoke. It's as elusive as it is essential. As personal as it is universal. Which makes writing a book about it delightfully difficult.

The most widely accepted definition is that creativity is the process of combining two separate things to produce something original and useful. For the purpose of this book, let's start there.

Our intention is to become masterful at remixing and repurposing the world around us into something useful, meaningful and *beautiful*.

And why 'everyday'? As Annie Dillard famously said, 'How we spend our days is, of course, how we spend our lives'. It's easy to get swept up in grandiose visions of big projects, global domination and org-wide transformation. But the biggest dreams and most beautiful working lives are built on the back of small, conscious and consistent actions.

But to be clear, we're not necessarily talking about art here. We won't be working on your watercolour technique or practising scales on the guitar (unless you choose to). Having said that, if during our discovery you decide that your future lies on Broadway, I'm all for it. But our focus is on developing a mindset that has:

≈ a natural bias for the new and the next

≈ the courage to consistently choose alternate possibilities over predictable approaches

≈ the discipline to do it every single day, in the smallest and largest of ways.

The underlying essence of this book, however, is that you will come to define what creativity is for *you*. You'll decide, through your own lived experience, what it is, why it matters and how best to use it.

By exploring the ideas and exercises presented in these pages, you'll have the tools to rewrite your own relationship with creativity. You'll start to redesign your life so that you can more easily access it. And begin to reimagine the infinite number of ways you can apply it in your work and career to tremendous effect.

Ready?

Choose your own adventure

First, I want you to understand why this book is different, and why it's *dangerous* ...

Most books on creativity fail to demonstrate how fundamental it is for success and fulfilment in business *and* life. Nor do they express the urgency with which I believe all of us should be pursuing our own creative sensibilities.

They often leave readers with little more than a few tired platitudes, a bunch of boring anecdotes, and a handful of generic 'brainstorming activities' (that almost always involve coloured markers and post-it notes).

This book is different. It doesn't attempt to reduce or generalise the creative process. Because creativity can't be reduced to a generalised process. It's subjective, idiosyncratic and infinite. And besides, despite my best efforts to help get you there ...

finding your way back to your creativity is itself an act of creativity.

Your journey will be different from mine. Which makes it all the more meaningful. Therefore, it's best to think about this book as a series of provocations, not prescriptions. There is no 'one way' to read it, and no 'right outcome' as a result of it. However you feel and whatever you create while reading, it's entirely personal and reassuringly perfect.

Every exercise or example is taken from my own lived experience or the experiences of people I know and trust. People who found the courage to put a little more creativity into their life. A little more personality into their work. A little more humanity into their workplace.

You will have your own stories to tell. Your own roadblocks to overcome. Your own style of perceiving and processing the insights and inspiration you encounter. My recommendation is that you make the process of reading this book creative.

What does that mean?

It means scribble on the text, dog-ear the edges, tear out pages and make them into paper planes if you must. Get yourself a journal and rewrite passages you love in your own words. Draw pictures of the monsters that have been preventing you from creating. Write poems and songs and sonnets and short stories. Write business ideas, draw stage setups and design marketing plans as you go.

If you want this book to make a difference to you, you've got to make it work for you.

Just to reassure you, this book won't tell you to quit your job. It doesn't demand that you take up the violin or move to Berlin. But it will ask important things of you — things that might be uncomfortable to confront or inconvenient to apply. But that's why you're here, isn't it? To step beyond the obvious and into the outrageous. To leave the confines of convention and fully embrace your rare, radical and resplendent self.[1]

So let's get to the heart of it.

---

[1] How good is that word! If you, like me, might not have been fully up to speed with 'resplendent' until this moment, it means 'attractive and impressive through being richly colourful or sumptuous. To shine and to glitter'. Well, if that ain't the perfect description of you and your everyday creativity, I don't know what is.

This book is a cold shower wake-up call for people who want a more meaningful experience at work.

It's for the people who are tired of the uninspired, risk-averse, bureaucratic bullshit that is rife within most corporate workplaces. It's for the courageous few who have a deep desire to put more play into their work, more joy into their job and more meaning into the relationships they share with their colleagues and clients.

This book can be the answer to the question we've all been asking about our work: 'Is this it?'

When you commit to your creative recovery you become a powerful participant in a radical revolution. You'll join a colourful cast of misfits and mavericks, rebels and renegades, outsiders and originals who are changing how and why we work.

Don't for a second underestimate how important this is. We live in crazy times. The world is burning, the robots[2] are coming and the challenges we face are too fast and fierce for us to follow the rules.

The world we live in used to value those who could ace the test. The ones who could memorise information, master instruction and make exact replicas of the original. Now we have machines for that. Machines that don't need to be fed or need a break. Machines that don't get upset or ask for time off. They just produce, consistently and efficiently.

What the world values now are those of us who can dream. Those who can reinterpret and reinvent the world in new and exciting ways. To survive and thrive in the emerging economic landscape you must:

≈ reclaim your wild, untamed self-expression

≈ redefine your unique, authentic value

≈ rewrite the way you make a meaningful difference to those around you.

---

[2] And viruses! As this book goes to print, it's April 2020 and we're up to our eyeballs in the global COVID-19 pandemic.

A word of warning

There's a reason why the tagline of this book is 'a dangerous guide for making magic at work'.

Recovering your creativity is powerful. It changes you and the world around you. And change is unnerving. When I say 'dangerous' I mean it's dangerous for anyone or anything that is too small for the person you will become.[3]

It's dangerous for your boss (if you have one) because they will have to shift the way they see and value you. It's dangerous for your colleagues (if you have them) because they will have to evolve themselves with you. It's dangerous to your ego because you will have to think and act in ways that are outside what you know and have grown comfortable with.

But it's worth it. You weren't born to just tick boxes, await instruction or to simply follow the rules. None of us were. You were born to make things. To change things. To improve the world in all kinds of ways that only you can.

Now is the time. Now is *your* time: to remember, to realign with and to re-create who you are and how you're going to bring more beauty, intimacy and humanity to the world around you.

The future of work will be written by those with the courage to think, feel, act and be more creative, every day.

And if you're reading this, that means you.

Welcome to the ride of your life.

---

[3] To paraphrase a quote from the great poet and philosopher David Whyte.

How To Read This Book

The irony of writing a book about liberating your creativity then giving you advice on how to read it is not lost on me. So please, read this in whatever way serves you. All in one sitting or one sentence a day. Begin at the end or flip to any random page and start there. If you're ready to blaze away, by all means. Jump straight to chapter 1 or anywhere you like.

Having said that, I have tried to write it in a linear way that builds on previous chapters. So reading from start to finish is preferable. And I *really* encourage you to do the exercises and activities as they're designed—especially the ones that make you feel the most uncomfortable. The ones that take a lot of time. And the ones where the ROI is unclear to you.

Because that's where the change is: in doing the things you wouldn't normally do. Or the things you stopped doing long ago.

If something feels silly, pointless or insignificant, ask yourself: why? Try to decipher whether it's something you can confidently step over, or whether it's just another way for you to resist or avoid the very thing you came here for.

I want you to see this book as a sacred space of self-indulgence.

A lot of it you can do privately and quietly. No-one has to know. You won't look foolish or be exposed. But there are plenty of activities that specifically ask you to learn out loud. To declare your aspirations before you have a plan for how to fulfil them. To raise your hand before you have a question. To take the lead even if (especially if) you have no idea where you're leading us.

To get in the game.

Because that is where the magic happens. That is how you will speed up your creative recovery and begin to enjoy the limitless potential that comes from cultivating a creative life.

To make it easier, I've included 'bonus points' in every activity. This is how you can speed up your recovery. It might feel like a little too much to begin with. That's fine. You can come back to it later, once you've got a bit more wind in your sails.

I've also built an online portal that is full of more info and inspo to assist in your transformation. There are videos and interviews, along with a collection of worksheets that expand on the ideas presented in here.

You can find that by heading to **www.everydaycreatives.com** and signing up to the VIP section by using the code **IAMCREATIVE**. You'll gain lifetime access to all kinds of inspiring material.

And for the audiophiles, I've even created an audiobook that turns the format on its head. Being a musician by trade, I've called on a few of my friends, and together we've created an audiobook that feels more like an atmospheric 3D landscape, complete with soundtracks and effects, and real-life interviews with individuals featured in the book.

I want this book to leap up and out of these pages into your life. I want the ideas to become activated in your work and relationships. I want the potential of these paragraphs to be realised through you. I want you, like me, to become another instrument of change. Another vehicle for everyday creativity.

A smiling assassin finding magic in the mundane, putting extra into the ordinary, sautéing secrets into the special sauce.

Oooooh, I'm excited. Are you ready?

TIME TO PLAY
Cement Your intent

Alrighty then, let's get right to it. Put all these glorious aspirations into action and cement your intent. In this game, integrity is everything. To make and sustain change, your word matters. I'm now going to ask you to commit to this process. To do all the exercises within as they're designed and to hold yourself accountable for your own creative recovery.

It's time to make and sign your Creative Contract.

You can write yours in this book (I've left you a few blank pages), or fill in the blanks and sign the contract I've outlined on the following page. Or better yet, you could find an old typewriter from a secondhand store, write up your own contract, in your own words, on a sheet of recycled paper, sign it, frame it and hang it above your desk.

You can do anything, as long as you do *something*. I'm inviting you to start on the good foot, set the tone for our time together and get creative in *how* you commit to your creativity.

Creative Contract

I, _____ , am a natural born creative. There is no-one on the planet who has the expertise and experience that I have. I am a product of the infinite dance of choice and chance and it is my right and responsibility to bring all of my creative potential to my work, life and relationships.

I, _____ , understand that I've been heavily influenced by a world that sought to make me into a _____ . I understand that this process will kick my arse. It will demand that I confront long-held, limiting beliefs about who I am and what I'm capable of. I recognise that parts of my brain will _____ much of this process. It will justify and rationalise not doing most of the exercises I am asked to complete.

But I commit to doing them anyway. All of them. Because I am _____ .

I, _____ , have also decided this program must be _____ . If I'm going to finish it has to feel _____ . So I also commit to celebrating by _____ every time I complete a chapter, exercise or activity.

This is my time to shine, baby. Bring it on!

Signed _____

Date _____

BONUS POINTS

Done that? Excellent. Now I'm going to invite you to take this even further. To embody your intent by creating a threshold to cross.

Get some chalk and draw a line on the street outside your house. Or gather stones from the garden and arrange them in a line on your lawn. I'm asking you to create a 'line in the sand'.

Once you've done that, stand in front of this line, take a few deep breaths and fully commit to this process. Then when you're ready, step over that line and into the game we're playing.

If you're thinking, 'Whatever, Myke. You lost me already', might I remind you of the creative contract you just signed.[4] In this game your word is everything. Integrity matters. And this is far from frivolous.

It's an embodied expression of your intent. If you want to become an Everyday Creative you've got to move out of your head and into your hands and heart. You've got to bring your whole self to every opportunity. You've got to want to play.

This is a dance between you and your potential. If you can't draw a chalk line on a road and step over it **when no-one is watching**, how on earth are you going to share that bold, brilliant idea when you find yourself in the lift with the boss?

Everything in this book is intentional. Every moment you have is an opportunity to flex your Everyday Creativity. To do things you wouldn't normally do. *Especially* if they feel silly and inconsequential. It's not your job to question or resist these activities (though you will). It's your job to embrace and enjoy them. To make them your own. And for bonus points, to share them with others.

---

[4] Boom! Gotcha like the fine print on the nutrition app you signed up for on Instagram!

Still having trouble with the whole 'line in the sand' thing? Perhaps you're on a plane or reading in a meeting room? Loving that perfectly legitimate excuse you're hanging on to?

Here are your options:

1. Out and about? Then wait until you're at home or somewhere you're alone. In that case, close the book right now and go read something else. Or go back and read this introduction again.

2. In the air? Get out of your seat, walk to the back of the plane and stand in the galley. Borrow a pen from the flight attendant and draw a line on the spew bag from the back the seat. Place it on the ground, cement your intent, then step over it.

3. Bonus points for bringing a flight attendant along for the ride and stepping over it together.[5]

4. Triple bonus points for taking a photo of your feet as you cross your line in the sand and sending it to me at mykel@mykeldixon.com or posting it online with the hashtag #everydaycreative.

---

[5] You can see examples of people doing this in the online portal – www.everydaycreatives.com

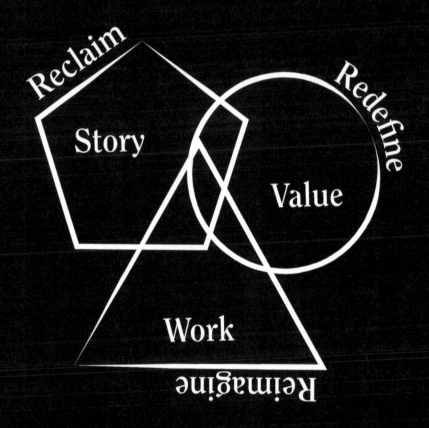

PART ONE

Preparing The Canvas

Before we start to create, we've got to prepare the canvas. We've got to clear some space, sharpen our tools and mix a few paints.

To do that, it's important we understand how we ended up here. We have to find out:

≈ why we find it so hard to be creative

≈ why our workplaces seem to crush any attempt to do things differently

≈ who might be to blame for the blockages we experience on a daily basis.

So take a few deep breaths, push your shoulders back and let us begin our voyage to the centre of your human potential.

CHAPTER ONE
An Identity Crisis

It's not your fault,
but it is your responsibility

'Myke, I love what you've got planned but I'm a little concerned. This might be a bit much for our people. Can we dial back the creative stuff a bit? We want them to be challenged but we don't want to make them uncomfortable.'

It was our fifth face-to-face meeting in as many months. The GM, HR director and L&D (learning and development) manager of a mid-sized accounting firm were sitting opposite me. We were once again crammed in a small windowless meeting room to discuss their upcoming conference (which I'd been engaged to design and facilitate). Aside from the pleasantries and a few logistical updates, this delightful group of leaders spent the vast majority of our conversation trying to lower my expectations of their people.

They seemed hell bent on reaffirming how 'un-creative' their team was. Fixated on their introversion. Obsessed with their bias for linear process. Anxious about their apparent inability to cope with anything 'outside the box'.

If my experience with people, both in and outside corporate life, has taught me anything, it's that everyone has a unique capacity for creativity. And when given the opportunity, placed in the right context and supported by the right conditions...

Even the most reserved, rational or risk-averse among us yearns to unleash their wild, untamed self.

'We'll be fine', I said. 'I have a feeling they're going to surprise you.'

Fast forward three weeks and it's 4.30 on a mild afternoon in May. We've just finished a two-day conference and I'm waving goodbye to a busload of enthusiastic auditors who are singing and high-fiving their way back to Melbourne.

Over the last 48 hours we covered all the usual business updates and strategic content. We heard from the executives and set renewed team targets. But there was something different about how we delivered the content: embedded in every session was a multitude of creative activations to get the delegates out of their heads and into their hands and hearts.

We had a live band in the centre of the main room for the entire first day. We held a film festival later that night that featured movies created by delegates. We left more room for reflection and discussion. We leveraged colour, natural light, physical movement and tactile activities. We asked a wider array of questions and frequently adjusted the agenda to follow the flow of every conversation.

I witnessed a group of supposedly shy, left-brain, analytical people step up to the metaphorical mic and sing. At various points over the two days, the group choreographed dance routines, directed and starred in short films, played musical instruments for the first time. They wrote their team strategy as a haiku, used the hallway furniture to map out their customer journey and performed the company's origin story as a live, improvised musical.

They started raising their hands before they were prompted, stopped asking permission to change the program, and became quite comfortable breaking any real or perceived rules when working on an interactive game or exercise.

Hidden creative talents surfaced among the most unlikely of individuals. Energy levels peaked and their ideas for new products, projects or processes were surprisingly polished. There was no way you could differentiate this group of auditors from a group of professional creatives.

Now before you get all, 'Yeah, sounds a bit kindergarten to me' or 'Sure, but where's the ROI? And how is that relevant to their day-to-day work?', well, you tell me! What difference would it make to *your* work if you:

≈ felt comfortable and enthusiastic when facing never-before-seen challenges

≈ could see and sense the desires of your clients from a new, expanded perspective

≈ felt deep trust and psychological safety among your teammates so that you feel confident being all of who you are, all of the time?

The example I just shared was a unique experience for that company but it was far from rare for me. I see it over and over again. Across industries, functions, nationalities, gender. Boomers or Millennials. Creativity doesn't discriminate.

In the weeks following an event like that I will always receive private and group messages from participants on email or LinkedIn. I'll even get a phone call or two and they always sound like this:

≈ 'Myke, thank you, I haven't had that much fun in years.'

≈ 'It was so great to get to know everyone on such a personal level. I feel so much more connected to my team and I had no idea how much talent there is among us.'

≈ 'I really miss expressing myself like that. It reminds me how important it is to make time for this stuff.'

≈ 'I can see a whole new way of working within my role. I have so many new ideas and feel so much more confident being bold and audacious.'

Then a few months after that, I'll start getting tagged online in projects those people and teams have deployed. I'll hear stories about the changes that have taken place in the office. The humanising of internal processes, the personalising of the customer experience, the electrifying enthusiasm that the team has been riding and applying to their work.

I literally have hundreds of these messages and it's astonishing how quickly the impact starts to show. Incredibly, this kind of impact doesn't just take place on two-day retreats or a year-long creative leadership program. It can happen in a 30-minute keynote.

Compelled to close the conference

Here's an email verbatim, from a beautiful guy named Gary who I met during an event. We had a spontaneous live debate during my keynote about the merit and magic of creativity, and trusting my intuition I invited Gary onto stage to close the entire conference by sharing his perspective with a room full of strangers (while I accompanied him on piano).[6]

Subject Line: Rip off the beige and run down the street naked

Dear Mykel,

Many, many thanks for unleashing my inner emotions today. Often these corporate events are so formulated and you breathed a breath of fun and creativity and intelligence and fear (for me!) to end the day.

Your stats and research resonated with me so much I had to pipe up. I love my family deeply (wife, 13-year-old twins — one of each — and an 11-year-old son), but I'm in a constant battle with my

---

[6] You can see images of the precise moment Gary jumped on stage in the VIP section of the online portal—www.everydaycreatives.com

13-year-old daughter trying to get her to conform and fit in — she is incredibly creative (not sure where she gets it from!), and will look at every opportunity to buck conformity.

My wife studies positive psychology and neuroscience, and has tried in vain to get me to understand the value of our daughter's creativity and free spirit. Mykel you challenged and converted me in 30 thoroughly enjoyable short minutes. If you've done one thing today you've converted a stoic, by-the-book rule-bound father to remember his childhood and become a five-year-old again. Think Tom Hanks in Big ... in reverse.

Keep doing what you're doing, and shaking the tree. Love your work, and I look forward to reading your book.

Big love back at you brother,

Gary (or Gaaaarrrry)

I'm so fortunate I get to observe this flourishing of the human spirit on a weekly basis. People who believe wholeheartedly that they aren't creative (or aren't anymore) reconnect with the creative spark within them. And within days, weeks or months they transform their work and life in ways they couldn't have imagined.

Now, I'm not telling you this to stroke my ego, but rather because to me, it's abundantly clear:

We don't have a creativity crisis, we have an identity crisis.

We're not struggling against a lack of creative talent. We're suffocating beneath a misguided story. Drowning in a dangerous delusion that we're not who we naturally are and don't have what we've naturally got.

We're adrift in a sea of lies about who we are and what we think we're capable of.

So when did we adopt such a limiting view of our creative potential? And who or what is to blame for such a disempowering narrative?

Well, to understand that, we've got to go back a hundred years to the second industrial revolution and a man by the name of Frederick Winslow Taylor.

Blame Tay Tay

Taylor was a curious man. He spent his early career working in the steel industry. And while observing what he described as 'gross inefficiencies among workers', he became interested in how an organisation could improve its productivity.

In 1902, he published a paper known as 'The Principles of Scientific Management'. In it, he proposed that companies could massively improve their productivity by applying a scientific method to their work. By separating and simplifying every stage of production; by training unskilled workers to perform specialised sequences of tasks; and by closely monitoring and measuring every aspect of a job, organisations could optimise their output and increase their profit.

Under Scientific Management, workers were never encouraged to make their own decisions or evaluate any actions that might produce a better result. In fact, they were forbidden to. They were even punished when they did. Taylor was known for having no concern whatsoever for the satisfaction or motivation of workers; he cared only about the company's output. Charming.

Before Taylor showed up, work was mostly performed by skilled craftspeople. They learned their profession through lengthy apprenticeships and often took vast amounts of time to produce their best work. They made their own decisions about how to perform their job (agency). They developed their own expertise through experience and experimentation (learning agility). And they were mostly responsible for the entire process of production (ownership).

Scientific Management, however, gave companies a way to produce at a speed and scale like never before. They could employ more people with very little knowledge or experience, train them to complete a specific task that was easily monitored and measured, and replace them without losing productivity (or profits).

(Sheesh, I bet he was popular at Friday night drinks.)

Let's look at the four principles of Scientific Management in a little more detail. You tell me if anything sounds or feels familiar:

1. Replace 'rule of thumb' methods with 'scientific methods' to determine the 'one best way' to compete each and every task (i.e. remove all autonomy, disregard previous expertise and prioritise data over human experience).

2. Scientifically select, train and develop each worker rather than leaving them to train themselves (i.e. define a job description then find a worker to fit into it; train employees to become competent in their specific tasks, not competent life-long learners capable of mastering multiple tasks).

3. Cooperate with workers to ensure that the scientifically developed methods are being followed (i.e. micromanage everything, performance review everything else and ensure KPIs are embedded everywhere).

4. Divide work between management and labour so that managers can plan and train while workers perform and execute (i.e. build a bureaucracy, establish a hierarchy and maintain the division of silos).

Make no mistake, we're living in the long tail of the industrial era. A time during which workers were made to be machines. A time that robbed us of our freedom to think for ourselves, explore alternate possibilities and produce work that was personally meaningful to us.

But that's only half the story. The rewiring of our natural creative capability and the adoption of an unnatural identity began long before we entered the workforce.

School's out

Ten years before Taylor released his principles of Scientific Management, there was a group of scholars and educators in the United States called The Committee of Ten. They were led by the then-president of Harvard, and in 1892 established the standardised form of education most of the world adopted and still uses today.

The Committee of Ten were the first folks to decide on the optimal size of a class. The ideal layout of a classroom. The most suitable subjects to fill a curriculum. They separated students by age and determined what subjects should be introduced at what year level.[7] They installed methods to monitor and measure a student's progress and performance by way of testing and examination.

Wait a second. Does any of that sound familiar? It's almost as though we educate our kids the same way we run our factories.

We sort and separate the raw materials (kids). We introduce new parts (subjects) at different stages of production (year levels). We test, measure and evaluate the product at each stage of the process to ensure there are no defects (exams). And with one last tick of approval from the regulators (final exam results), the finished product is ready to hit the shelves (graduation).[8]

I like to believe the intention of the Committee of Ten was noble — to give more people access to education and elevate the employability of society — but there were unintended consequences.

---

[7] For example — geography in year seven, biology in year ten.

[8] These ideas have been articulated by many leading scholars, most notably by the brilliant Sir Ken Robinson in his book *The Element* (required reading).

What we teach matters, but not nearly as much as how we are taught to learn.

Beyond literacy and numeracy, history and biology, what we really learned at school was how to conform. How to prioritise what's being measured, not what we find interesting. How to colour inside the lines, not make a mosaic on the walls. How to sit quietly and await further instruction, not proactively pursue our passion.

To put it bluntly, we were reprimanded and punished anytime we were creative. In a study called 'Creativity: Asset or Burden in the Classroom?', elementary school teachers were asked to rate their favourite students and rate each student's creative capability. The researchers found that students displaying creative characteristics were the most unappealing to teachers.

And as Adam Grant points out in his *New York Times* best-selling book, *Originals*,

> Teachers tend to discriminate against highly creative students. Labelling them as troublemakers. In response, many children quickly learn to get with the program, keeping their original ideas to themselves. In the language of author William Deresiewicz, they become the world's most excellent sheep.

When we're taught there's only one correct answer, we're robbed of our ability to seek and hold multiple truths. When we're taught that success goes to those who can memorise the most information, we learn to retain only what will be on the test. When we or our peers are punished for speaking up or speaking out, we decide the safest thing to do is to keep our head down, do what we're told and wait for the bell to ring.

Replication over **originality.**

Memorisation over **imagination.**

Conformity over **curiosity.**

Efficiency over **experimentation.**

Perfection over **play.**

Compliance over **defiance.**

Buttering up the teacher over **speaking truth to power.**[9]

Although there's a growing movement of visionaries advocating sweeping educational reform, we still have a long way to go. And I'm certainly not trying to throw shade at the people who currently work within it. Teachers, in my opinion, are grossly undervalued and, given the constraints and pressure they're under to deliver, they're doing a phenomenal job.[10]

I just want you to be crystal clear on all the ways the world has influenced you to become the person you are.

You've been heavily conditioned to believe the things you believe about what is valuable and what is possible.

_____

[9] No prizes for guessing why I had such a hard time at school. What about you?

[10] If you're thinking, 'But my kids are doing all sorts of awesome things at school', I'd like to point out Australia's education system is currently ranked 39 out of 41 of the world's developed nations. And our current focus on STEM is misguided as it doesn't fully appreciate the speed and power of our technology. Soon algorithms will be building algorithms far better than we can. If you want to prepare your kids for the future, immerse them in the arts and humanities. Entrepreneurship and emotional intelligence. But more on this later…

And it doesn't stop there. What about the stereotypical narratives we're bombarded with every day?

Unhelpful stereotypes

Hollywood has long presented artists and creatives as flaky, unshaven, and self-absorbed. Born talented, lived alone, died poor. Destined to a life of extravagance or destitution.

Over the last few centuries, we were told to see science, logic and reason as the preferred apparatus for progressing our world,[11] while art, emotion and intuition have been relegated to merely decoration or entertainment.

We were told we're either left-brained or right-brained, a myth first made popular in 1979 by the book *Drawing on the Right Side of the Brain* by Betty Edwards. The concept has since been proven to be a gross reduction of the brain's capabilities.

And let's not forget the endless array of personality tests and strengths diagnostics that love to pigeonhole us as either creative or non-creative by way of a series of inane, leading questions.

---

[11] Due in part to the influence of Aristotle and the lingering residue of the Enlightenment.

13

We don't care what she does.
Medicine, finance or law,
it's her choice…

Art?

Is it any wonder we have a dysfunctional relationship with our creativity? Or why so many parents nudge their kids away from a life in the arts toward the safety and security of medicine, finance and law?

But it's often so much more than the desire for a more respectable, affluent lifestyle that stands in the way. Most of us have deep, psychological trauma that keeps us from going anywhere near our latent creativity.

Battle scars

During a podcast with Elizabeth Gilbert (author of *Big Magic*), Brené Brown, the best-selling author of countless books on vulnerability, and the world's foremost expert on shame, said something that really struck me.

In Brown's research on shame, she revealed 85 per cent of people have a significant emotional scar from childhood. Something that cut so deep it shaped how they came to view themselves and their place in the world. Which in turn shaped the decisions they made and the life they came to live.

Of that 85 per cent, 50 per cent were scarred as a result of direct shaming around creativity. They were told they couldn't sing. That they looked stupid when they danced. That their writing was terrible. That their ideas were dumb, wrong or not good enough. And that's all it took. One throwaway comment from a teacher, relative, stranger or friend and we put away the paint, for good.

Our brains have instinctively shaped our identity to protect ourselves from further psychological trauma. Once bitten, twice shy.

For so many of us, our creativity has been contaminated by feelings of shame. And like any sane person, we will do whatever we can to avoid feeling that way again. To be laughed at, ridiculed or ostracised for daring to dance — it's just not worth it. To engage with our creativity is to reopen the wounds that have defined our sense of self.

Um ... no thanks.

It's safe to say, we've all got a significant psychological handicap when it comes to our relationship with creativity.

Any good news?

The good news (ah finally, some good news!) is that, despite the influence of our education, our work environment and our childhood, we are, in fact, biologically designed to create.

Thanks to radical advances in neuroscience, there is a growing body of research that confirms all of us are born with roughly the same capacity for creativity. And the factors that determine whether we retain it later in life come down to environment and encouragement, not God-given talent or a genetic predisposition.

But the best research, which proved once and for all that we were always intended to create, was done decades ago. And it all began with the mother of all moonshots: our attempt to reach for the stars.

Born to create

Back in the 1960s, right after JFK declared the United States was going to put humans on the moon, NASA realised they would need an army of unbelievably gifted individuals to make it happen. They turned to a guy named George Land to help them find the boldest, brightest and most brilliant minds to complete the grandest mission of all time.

He created a test that measured the creative capacity of an individual and an individual's ability to access their creativity. And, as we all know, it was a pretty effective test. Somehow, that collective of wildly creative humans pulled off a rather large miracle.[12]

Once the champagne had worn off and he had stopped receiving so many party invitations, George had to decide what project he'd take on next. He recalled his infamous creativity test and, on a whim, decided to try it on a bunch of five-year-olds.

---

[12] Unless you don't believe we ever made it to the moon. Right on. We're all about diversity and inclusion here. And I love a good conspiracy theory after a few wines. So you keep on believing whatever works for you!

So he gathered over 1600 little cherubs and gave them the exact same test he'd given the astrophysicists and engineers, the psychologists and lunar specialists.

The results revealed a staggering 98 per cent of five-year-olds could be classed as creative geniuses. They exhibited the same level of creativity as the most innovative minds at NASA — the ones that put us on the moon in 1969.

Keep in mind, these children weren't from NASA's school for the gifted. They weren't playing the violin with one hand while cooking a risotto with the other, speaking Mandarin and Cantonese at the same time, like my boys.

They were ordinary, everyday kids. Snotty noses, grubby knees. Kids, I assume, like you and I once were.

So, astounded by the results, George decided to make his test into a longitudinal study. He brought the same focus group of kids back to do the same test, under the same conditions, five years later. So now they're 10 years old.

Have a guess what percentage of kids could now be classed as creative geniuses.

Is it:

a)   80 per cent

b)   95 per cent

c)   30 per cent

d)   65 per cent

The answer? Well, you'll have to look in the footnote.[13]

He measured them again at 15. Same kids, same test, same conditions, and guess what? The number dropped again, this time to 12 per cent.? He measured one more time. Now they're 30 years old and many have

_____

[13] The answer was 30 per cent — thanks for playing along!

kids of their own (again, like many of us!). The results showed that only 2 per cent of participants could be classed as brilliantly creative. George went on to say: 'The research is conclusive: non-creative behaviour is learned.'

Let's just take a minute to let that sink in. Ninety-eight per cent of us are born with an ability to access our limitless creativity. And by the time we turn 30, only 2 per cent of us exhibit the same natural creativity we were born with.

Ouch.

Here's the skinny

We were all schooled to follow the rules. Trained to be cogs in a wheel. Wounded by careless words and bombarded with harmful messages that told us being creative would leave us:

≈ misunderstood

≈ isolated

≈ poor.

We hero worship those who have retained and expressed their creativity in the arts and humanities. In science, tech, business and beyond. But the vast majority of us have adopted the disempowering story that we are not privy to the same innate sensibilities of those gifted few.

Our lives have been shaped by a set of beliefs that we embraced to help us navigate the uncertainty of our childhood or the uncomfortable nature of our workplace. As Seth Godin puts it, 'We have embraced the industrial propaganda with such enthusiasm that we have changed the very nature of our dreams'.

If you don't feel like an Everyday Creative, it's not your fault, but reclaiming it is your responsibility.

If we're going to recover your innate creativity, we've got to go straight to the source: head for the jugular and start with your identity. We've got to rewrite the story of you, for you.

This is why most creativity training doesn't work or doesn't last. It doesn't address the root cause. It merely dances around the surface, posturing with post-it notes or word association exercises. You can do all the creative capability training in the world, but if it's just a bandage stuck over a deeply entrenched story that you're not creative and never will be, how effective do you think it will be?

Now we're going to determine how you currently identify with creativity. By doing so, this will help address the entrenched narratives you've absorbed and give you a clear picture of what stops you from becoming the Everyday Creative you were born to be.

Used to be

Never was

Kinda
sorta

Love to be

Natural
born

Everyday

The six creative identities

Most people see themselves as one of six creative identities. Each specific domain leads to particular behaviours that reaffirm the existing narrative. But all can be transformed and transcended by following the practices in this book.

I'll briefly outline the six identities, but I recommend heading over to www.everydaycreatives.com. You'll find more detail on each of the six identities as well as an interactive diagnostic tool to uncover which personality you currently identify with.

1. Never Was Creative

These folks are by far the most deluded. They wholeheartedly believe that, of all the people on the planet, despite all the research I just took you through, they 'haven't got a creative bone in their body'. They chose a career that reflects this belief. Even if they ended up in a creative industry, they have made sure the work they actually do is anything but.

Perhaps they never had access to anything creative as a child. Or the environment they grew up in didn't value creativity. Maybe they had a sibling who excelled early on in a particular creative pursuit, which resulted in their family labelling them 'more of a sporty type'. Or 'the left-brained one'. And so they went along with it, accepted their role and chose a more conventional path.

Ironically, this group are often most at peace with their perceived (but unproven) lack of creativity. They marvel at those who express themselves creatively, and are eager to support any creative projects or people, but will never put themselves or their ideas forward. It's not necessarily through fear of failure, but through absolute acceptance that they couldn't possibly have anything creative to contribute.

2. Used To Be Creative

This group of creatives are the most heartbreaking and heartbroken. They have a creative past. They cared deeply about something, but at some point they were burned, scared and wounded for life. So much so, it's easier for them to lock up their creative desires and throw away the key.

But of course, they can't. And it claws at them. They see others creating and want so badly to be a part of it but their fear of getting hurt again stops them from jumping in the ring.

If left unchecked, Used To Be Creatives can be quite dangerous. As a reaction to their own unrealised potential, they can unconsciously seek to sabotage any creative projects or people, lashing out or passive-aggressively blocking any meaningful progress.

They, like the Never Was, believe creativity is something others do and are. And that they are no longer allowed or able to enjoy or experience its benefits.

3. Kinda Sorta Creative

Kinda Sorta Creatives are fence-sitters. They probably played an instrument for a few years in school, or occasionally indulge in something 'creative' as an adult (like a cooking class with hubby or helping a neighbour renovate their granny flat). But they like to stick with what they're good at.

They'll always wait for others to go first or choose an activity they've done before to ensure they don't look foolish. They enjoy creative pursuits and love to be a part of innovative projects but their preference is to fly beneath the radar. They're happy to be on a winning team, but not as captain, and preferably not holding the ball when there's 10 seconds to go and they're two points behind.

Deep down, Kinda Sorta Creatives know that their desire to be close to creativity will never be enough. They live in a constant state of inner conflict. They want to tear down the walls, rip off their clothes and cut loose, but they hesitate and wait: for a better time, for a partner in crime, or when they can be sure no-one else is watching.

4. Love To Be Creative

Simply put, Love To Be Creatives love to be creative. They know it's something they're capable of and they enjoy bringing it to their work and life. It's just that they're so focused on doing everything else right now that they can't seem to find the time. They look forward to when the workload eases, or when a new project opens up more opportunities to express themselves. Next week, next quarter or next year.

Their work ethic is admirable but they're victims of a misguided belief that getting more done will lead them to more success. They've adopted the 20th-century story of productivity and efficiency so thoroughly, they've forgotten that their advantage is both the thing they love and the thing they're good at: creativity.

Love To Be Creatives always express their natural creativity on a team offsite or at a leadership retreat. They're the first to volunteer and will often have the most innovative or hilarious suggestions during group activities. But all that creative potential fades the moment they step back into the office. And with it the respect, intimacy and connection they'd built with others by revealing more of themselves.

5. Natural Born Creative

Natural Born Creatives are those fortunate fools who slipped through the net of our industrial influence. They somehow retained their innate creativity and have no problem expressing it whenever and however they see fit.

They're a vital asset to any team or organisation thanks to their effortless ability to think differently. Through their unique approach they inspire others to more innovative action. But they can often fall victim to their own success.

Because creativity comes so naturally to them, they can often take it for granted. They might unknowingly hoard their ideas, snub someone's first attempt or become lazy with creative opportunities. And their individual talent doesn't translate so easily to group success: the people around them might initially marvel at their natural talent but will eventually overlook them in favour of someone who is more willing to show up consistently, act inclusively and contribute more meaningfully to the whole.

6. Everyday Creative

Which brings us to the Everyday Creatives: the fabulous fine folk who have made it their mission to bring small and large moments of creativity to their work and life every single day.

These people have plenty of wounds and scars from childhood. They might have a bit of natural talent, but their real talent lies in their ability to be courageous. To keep asking bigger, broader and more beautiful questions. To keep stepping over the fear of being laughed at or locked out of the boardroom. To keep doing the best they can with what they've got to help others recover their own relationship with their creative potential.

Everyday Creatives don't do what they do for recognition or reward. They're not following orders or starting a global movement. They're merely acting from their own truth, listening for and leveraging their own unique expertise and experience to bring more light, love and laughter to the moments that matter.

▲ ▲ ▲

Where are you on the spectrum? Where would you like to be? Wherever you are, you're now on the path to becoming an Everyday Creative. And since the biggest roadblock to our creativity is the story we tell ourselves *about* ourselves, that's where we'll begin. By writing our own Creative Manifesto.

TIME TO PLAY
Your Creative Manifesto

Organisations spend an awful lot of time (and money) trying to write their reason for being. It's sometimes called a mission statement, a vision statement or a declaration of intent. And it's important: it acts as their compass, lighthouse and anchor to shape and sustain their desired culture while giving them the clarity and confidence to fulfil their strategic objectives.

We're going to do the same, *but for you*. You're going to create a living document that clearly articulates who you are, what you're here to create and why it matters. You're going to make your own **Personal Creative Manifesto**.

The best manifestos function as both a statement of principles and a bold, sometimes rebellious, call to action. It should make you evaluate the gap between the principles that matter to you and your current reality. It should challenge assumptions you have about your creative capability, foster a deep commitment to your creative recovery, and provoke lasting, meaningful change to your identity.

Simply put, your manifesto is a statement of creative ideals and intentions. It is a powerful catalyst that will push you beyond your comfort zone and hold you accountable to your continuing creative flourishing.

If you want to change your identity (and you do), creating a personal manifesto is a great place to start.

Writing a Personal Creative Manifesto (and living by it) can have a tremendous impact on the way you are at work. If you're someone who knows what you stand for and the difference you intend to make, you'll inevitably stand out (whether you want to or not). Clarity of purpose is magnetic, distinct and rare.

So let's have some fun with it. Remember, this is for you. You don't ever have to show anyone. So go for it.[14]

Now it's your turn.

1. Write down all the things you believe to be true about creativity (from an aspirational perspective). All the things you love about creativity. All the ways it makes your life better.

2. Write all the things that you have learned while living your life. Everything that stands out to you. The principles, the mottos, the adages. What are the attitudes and beliefs that serve you well when life goes a little pear-shaped?

3. Finally, ask yourself: 'What is the change I'm seeking to make?' How are you going to make a dent on the world? What will people say about you once you're gone, dead and buried?

---

[14] If you're feeling like it's a little too soon to start declaring who you are and what kind of magic you're going to make, just go with it. You can return to this at any point during the book. In fact, I recommend it. Keep it alive. Keep tweaking it, testing it, trying things on. The more you give your attention to rewriting an empowering story regarding your creativity, the more effortlessly creativity will start to bleed into your life.

Once you've done that, spend some quality time playing with each phrase. Expand and contract each sentence. How does it feel to say out loud? How does each sentence feel in relation to the others? Are these statements best delivered in sequential order or a random flow of expressions?

Keep coming back to this. You don't have to do it in one sitting (but rock on if you do!). You can sleep on it. Leave it for a week. But commit to having it done by the end of this book.

I've left you room on the following two pages to scribble a few ideas right now. But make your finished product something far grander. Something that's a match for the miracle of creativity that you are.[15]

Three things to keep in mind

1. I recommend writing in short declarative statements. There is power in brevity. It makes your manifesto easier to remember and recall when you need it most.

2. You're not just defining where you're going, you're defining where you're coming from, cultivating a meaningful context for you to operate in and create from. A set of tenets, values or principles that anchor you to who you are and hope to become.

3. Make sure it doesn't become a 'set and forget' kind of document. I strongly recommend making a physical artefact to hold your creative manifesto.

---

[15] I've included a bunch of examples of manifestos in the online portal—www.everydaycreatives.com. Use them as inspiration if you're stuck, but remember this is your manifesto. It could be seven words or seven hundred. It could rhyme or it could be a story. It could be full of big, fancy words, or full of colourful, intricate pictures. Make it your own. Use this exercise in reclaiming your creative identity as an exercise in creativity.

BONUS POINTS

What if you cut out letters from magazines and made your document look like a ransom note? Then hung it over your desk in a frame you found in an op shop?

Or what if you wrote your manifesto with a permanent marker all over a mannequin, giving it a full body text-tattoo with meaningful messages scawled across the torso (kinda like Guy Pearce in the film *Memento*)?

Or what if you wrote a spoken-word piece, and recorded it over a video montage with a soundtrack to match? Perhaps it could even become the cover letter for the next position you apply for.

Take your manifesto out of your head, off the page and into your life. You can check out mine on the next page.

Myke's manifesto

I am a man, son, brother, friend
An artist, poet, storyteller and musician
I am a lover of love and a believer of dreams
A warrior, wanderer, barefoot gypsy

I am whoever I say I am
The product of my imagination
The result of my consistent action
A multidimensional manifestation
I am an inspiration, if not to anyone,
at least unto myself

I am the context from which I feel the world
And the content that I create for it
I am the headline and the fine print
And I reserve the right to redefine who I am
every single day.

I came here to dance, to dream, to play
To love, to give, to make
To seek, to strive, to will, to thrive
To drink, touch and taste every experience
I am blessed enough to receive.

I came here to explore, embrace and express
The infinite creative potential that I am
And to serve the sacred intention from where I came
I vow to bring light, love, truth and beauty
to each and every breath.
I do what I do to show my gratitude.

To honour the gift that I am who I am,
at this time, in this place

To join the galaxy of human stars who already shine
So that others, including myself,
may find their way to a better place.

I do this because I can.

Because I have an ability
and an opportunity to make magic
And it would be both wasteful
and disrespectful to do anything else.

I am an Everyday Creative.

Your manifesto

CHAPTER TWO

The Obstacle Is The Way

Make your work
a work of art

Imagine you're driving a Mustang convertible on a five-lane freeway at no more than 20 kilometres per hour. You're surrounded by thousands of other cars, filled with people who look just like you. Everyone is jostling for position, switching in and out of lanes, never really progressing.

Your boss is sitting next to you, shouting loudly and at length about the party you're heading to. They keep describing how important it is you get there on time and how incredible it will be when you arrive.

The car's GPS, which has the party's coordinates locked in, keeps beeping at you to get off the freeway and head to the outer suburbs. But whenever you attempt to exit, the boss tells you to stay in your lane. 'Just keep going a little while longer', they say, 'We'll get the next one'.

With every extra kilometre that you're trapped on that freeway, the soul-crushing repetition, frustrating mixed messages and suffocating lack of agency begin to take their toll. You switch on the cruise control. You switch off your passion for the promise of the party. You tune out of your boss's one-way conversation and tune in to what you have planned for the weekend.

Despite the increasing number of street signs you pass that say 'wrong way', 'freeway end ahead', 'continue at your own risk', you just keep on driving. Maintaining compliance. Accepting your fate. Resigned to the road ahead.

Sound familiar? This is how a friend of mine described their day-to-day experience at work: drowning in corporate rhetoric, locked in a holding pattern, forever circling the same terrain at a snail's pace.

Maybe your current situation isn't quite so dire, but I'm sure you can relate to that experience. In fact, I can almost guarantee you've had moments or seasons at work that feel just like that. Why? Because I meet people all the time, across multiple industries, at every level and function of an organisation, who admit to feeling the same way. Maybe not at first, but definitely after a few wines and always out of earshot of their executive.

Let's just call a spade a spade.

The way we work isn't working for us, it's working against us.

The consequences of this kind of environment are vast, but I'd like to focus on three trends that are the most damaging and pervasive.

Problem #1: Disengagement

According to ongoing reports by Gallup (the world's leading analytics firm), over 80 per cent of employees are *still* not engaged at work. Despite considerable investment in enhancing the employee experience, the dial has barely moved in a decade.

So what does 'engaged' even mean? It means three out of four people are not inspired at your work. They're doing just enough to keep from being fired and likely won't ever do more than what they're employed to do. For the vast majority of us, our jobs are nothing more than a pay cheque. A stopgap. Or an extended break between weekends.

That might not be you. You might be one of those rare creatures who loves their work. Who feels connected to their colleagues and is bringing their savvy, soulful self to every sticky situation. But statistically speaking, you're surrounded by people who aren't. And, as much as we don't like to admit it, we're heavily influenced by our environment.

You might be a passionate, purpose-driven person, but when you're among people who don't think, dream or care, it's contagious. It's hard to keep the flame alive when everyone around you is trying to blow it out.

Think back to when you first started at your current job. Did you have wild ambitions to make a difference? Were you eager to connect with new colleagues and excited to get stuck into more meaningful projects?

How long did it take for you to start compromising? To learn all the unspoken ways that 'things get done around here', to decipher who to avoid and who to butter up?

How long before you slid into cruise control and started plotting your next career move or planning your annual leave?

Problem #2: Disconnection

One of the great tragedies of modern times is how we've become so isolated from one another. Be it through technology or ideology, we are living in what George Monbiot calls 'The Age of Loneliness'.

In 2018, the Australian Loneliness Report found that 50 per cent of Australians professed to feeling lonely each week. The World Economic Forum reported that 40 per cent of people under 25 are isolated and one in four Millennials concede to not having a single friend. The UK even appointed a Minister for Loneliness to address the nine million people who report often or always feeling lonely.[16]

---

[16] There have been calls in Australia to do the same.

Given that loneliness has been linked with higher blood pressure and heart disease, you could say that it's literally breaking our hearts.

This means that there's a significant number of people working alongside you who don't feel connected to you. Or anyone. And there's nothing sadder than feeling alone in a crowded room.

Of course, not everyone believes that work should be full of best friends and deep and meaningfuls. Some people have no desire to socialise, build a friendship group or get to know their colleagues. But it's well documented that diverse and inclusive cultures are more productive and innovative. People who feel connected to the people around them report higher levels of purpose and fulfilment at work. And it's been proven that teams who socialise perform better than those that don't.

So quick poll—circle your answer

How much do you really know about the people you work with?

    a)   I know the time and place they fell first in love

    b)   I know their coffee preference

    c)   I (sometimes) remember their first name

How many of your LinkedIn connections have you taken out for coffee?

    a)   14

    b)   3

    c)   Still haven't completed my LinkedIn profile

When was the last time you said hello to a stranger in a lift? Attempted a little meaningful conversation? (Or even made eye contact?)

    a)   Yesterday

    b)   3 months ago

    c)   The night of my sisters wedding (after 2 bottles of champagne)

Problem #3: Disillusionment

But by far the most troubling trend in the world today is our general sense of disenchantment. The polarised political climate, the ongoing destruction of our natural environment and the severe lack of justice we see on a daily basis mean our trust in government, business and humanity is taking a beating.

Oil spills and opioids. Sexual misconduct, the abuse of power and the relentless exploitation of our personal data. We're witnessing an eroding faith in capitalism, a lack of confidence in democracy and a growing distrust of those we've chosen to lead us.

When we see the same people getting promoted, regardless of their performance; when we're told that hard work matters but find out that who you know matters more; when we see the leaders of the largest institutions in the world break the law and get nothing more than a slap on the wrist, it's almost impossible not to feel like the system is rigged. We can be forgiven for losing hope.

The danger is that our frustration leads to apathy, and our apathy turns to cynicism. We feel powerless, with no option but to accept what is and choose to check out. Or worse, we adopt an attitude of 'if you can't beat 'em, join 'em'. Or in many cases, 'if you can't beat 'em, do the minimum, engineer a redundancy, enjoy a little gardening leave, then get a new role with a competitor when money's tight'.

But every time we do that, the status quo wins. The system that no longer serves us gets stronger. We become complicit in the whole damn thing. Business as usual, baby.

Who's in?

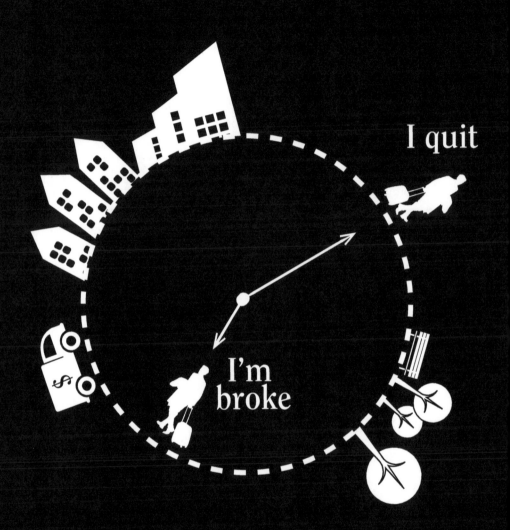

What if I told you there was another way?

A simple shift in mindset that opens the door to a new world of possibility. A subtle tweak in the way you see your circumstances that gives you more control over them. A powerful, practical and poetic pathway to put more joy into your job, more meaning into your meetings, and more beauty above and below the bottom line.

What if you didn't have to quit your job, sell all your stuff and travel through India on a nine-month sabbatical to remember (or re-create) who you are, what's important to you and where you want to go?

What if I told you that all the emails and WIPs,[17] the regulation and compliance, the drama and bureaucracy of the modern workplace are actually gifts? Creating a playground of possibility for exploring and expressing your fierce and fabulous self?

What if I told you that everything you need to transform your nine-to-five experience from 'getting through it' to 'let me at it' has been with you all along? That the seed of your superpower, the essence of your originality and the source of your salvation is at your fingertips?

It's called creativity, baby

Creativity is the key to your competitive advantage and the catalyst for transcending and transforming the world around you. This magical, mystical, marvellous thing has enabled us to evolve from walking apes to digital natives. Creativity is the source of all human progress. And it's all you need to carve out the career and life you desire and deserve.

When you begin to see the world through a lens of creativity, everything changes. Roadblocks and setbacks shift from feeling like a burden to feeling like an invitation. Annoying clients become alluring puzzles. Frustrating bureaucracy becomes a playful archnemesis: something that drives you forward, lifts you higher and compels you to be better at what you do.

---

[17] If you didn't get the acronym, WIP stands for 'Work In Progress', which are often weekly meetings to update teams on how things are going.

I believe creativity is the panacea for any and all challenges you face in the workplace. And I'm not the only one …

A new demand for creativity

In 2010 IBM interviewed over 1500 CEOs. They unanimously agreed that creativity is the number one factor for future business success. In 2018, The World Economic Forum placed creativity in the top three skills needed to thrive in the new world of work. And last year, LinkedIn conducted a deep analysis of what skills employers are now looking for in job candidates. Creativity came in as the number one 'soft' skill for the next decade. Though I'd hardly call it soft, especially when it delivers such hard returns.

Research by Adobe found that creative companies enjoy 1.5 times the market share. Brands that put creativity at the heart of their strategy have outperformed the S&P Index by 219 per cent over 10 years. Our friends at McKinsey have even developed a 'Creativity Index' whereby they can measure the creative capability of a company. The companies that score high on the index outperform their competitors in two key metrics:

1. an appetite and aptitude for innovation (growth)

2. shareholder return (profit).

That's right. Cold hard cash. Make no mistake,

creativity is now the strongest economic currency.

But all that ROI isn't limited to shareholders. In a global study called 'State of Create,' Adobe found that respondents who identify as 'someone who creates for a living' enjoyed 17 per cent higher household income than non-creators. And the Foundation for Young Australians in their 'The New Basics' report looked at the data of over 4.2 million job listings over three years, and found that any job that listed creativity as an attribute had an average annual salary boost of $3129.

(Alright, let's just take a minute for you to go update your LinkedIn profile. Put 'creative' in your job title and get some of that extra cash. You deserve it. I'll wait.)

A global shift

So that's what's going on now. But what about the future? Research by NESTA, an innovation foundation based in the UK, predicts an 87 per cent growth rate in the creative industries over the next 10 years. Compare this with the anticipated sharp decline in traditional roles and industries.[18]

And this accelerating demand for creativity is not limited to the West or the developed nations of the world. In 2015, the Indonesian government established 'The Creative Economy Agency' with a mandate to develop and harness the creative potential of their people. In 2018, they ran the world's first global conference on the creative economy and currently have four tech unicorns (companies valued over $1b). In comparison, Australia has one.

South Korea was named the world's best-equipped country to handle the effects of our changing global economy according to the Automation Readiness Index.[19] This is due to the government's sweeping reform of their education curriculum and teacher training, placing a heavy focus on soft skills and creativity.

And China is in the midst of a global rebrand from 'Made in China' to 'Designed in China', hoping to capitalise on the rise of the creative economy and transform their twentieth-century identity from a nation of producers to a nation of designers and makers.

The world is waking up to the limitless potential of creativity. And many forward-thinking leaders, companies and nations are already investing heavily in building their creative capacity to prepare for changes to our global economy.

So what's causing this sudden shift in focus from productivity and efficiency to creativity and empathy?

---

[18] And consider everything happening in 2020. At time of printing, we're all being asked to find alternative ways of working and living in response to the spread of COVID-19.
[19] The Automation Readiness Index assesses how well prepared countries are for the challenges and opportunities of intelligence automation.

The robots are coming!!!

Well, in reality, they're already here. We're living through the fourth industrial revolution, a global shift to a fully automated workforce. And anything that can be automated will be automated. Over the last few years we've seen A.I. lawyers outperform human lawyers, and A.I. doctors diagnose patients with more accuracy than human doctors. And Wall Street is now almost entirely run by algorithms.

In the 'Future of Jobs' report for 2018, the World Economic Forum predicted over 54 per cent of current employees will need significant re- and up-skilling by 2022. In Australia, the CSIRO in their report 'Tomorrow's Digitally Enabled Workforce' predicted 44 per cent of Australian jobs are under threat by the new industrial revolution. And many research institutes around the world suggest that most businesses are grossly unprepared for the inevitable transition to an artificially intelligent workforce.

So when smart machines control all the world's finances and run the factory floors, what will humans be left to do? We'll make art, says Kai-Fu Lee, a former Google and Microsoft executive and globally renowned AI expert:

Art and beauty are very hard to replicate with AI. Given AI is more objective, analytical, data driven, maybe it's time for some of us to switch to the humanities, liberal arts, and beauty.

This part of the story is missing from most media reports.

The robots aren't necessarily coming for your job; they're coming for the worst parts of your job, leaving you free to do more complex and creative work.

While smart machines might be better at processing and analysing old information, organisations today need people who can synthesise data and reimagine new possibilities. They need bold, brave and brilliant minds that consistently find and formulate new value. They need visionary, proactive and empathetic individuals who embrace ambiguity, thrive in uncertainty and seek out new opportunities to surprise and delight their customers.

They need Everyday Creatives — like you.

The opportunity

If you've been paying attention, you might've noticed the exciting opportunity that exists in this confluence of events.

The old way of working no longer works. At least not for humans. We've hit the limit on our capacity to do routine tasks, sit through boring meetings, and follow archaic rules and processes. As a result, we're disengaged, disconnected and disillusioned by the whole thing.

Simultaneously, our technology is slowly but surely eating away most of our routine tasks. The work that we were taught and measured on can now be done more effectively and efficiently by a computer. Increasingly, and somewhat ironically, the only work left for us to do is all the stuff we're naturally good at: creativity, complex problem solving, empathy, imagination, vision, sense-making, social intelligence, love.

And the demand for individuals who are fluent with these skills is growing exponentially.

So we have a choice to make:

≈ Keep doing what we've always done. Ride out this new wave of disruption and wait for instruction from those above or below us.

≈ Or begin to invest in our creative capacity. Redesign your work and life to support your continuing self-expression.

Circle your answer now (like seriously, get a pen and graffiti the page):

Keep doing what we've always done
OR
invest in your creative capacity?

From conflict to creativity

Any good author will tell you that the most fundamental element of a great story is *conflict*. It's the tension between where our hero is and where they want or need to be that drives the plot forward. And the bigger the challenge, the badder the enemy, the better the story.[20]

We love to hate the evil sister. We secretly crave the corrupt establishment. We want the weather to change, thwarting the hero's plans, pushing them beyond their limits (think Jim Carrey in *The Truman Show*).

Because, ultimately, we want to watch them overcome the trials and tribulations of the journey. We want to see everyday people unlock the extraordinary potential inside of them. We want to believe that maybe, just maybe, that potential is in us too.

So what does all this have to do with being an Everyday Creative and making magic at work?

You are that hero. You're dealing with conflict every single day.

The tension of where you are and where you want to be is what drives your story forward.

Just like every great hero, the only way you'll overcome the barriers that stand in your way is if you change. If you transcend your old identity and transform into the hero you were born to be.

---

[20] This idea is based on the brilliant work of Joseph Campbell. He was the world's foremost expert on myth and I thoroughly recommend checking out his seminal work, *The Hero's Journey*.

Now, before we go on, I get it. Calling yourself a hero is borderline repulsive for most people. And to be clear, I'm not giving you an excuse to behave like a hero at work. I'm not advocating narcissism or self-indulgence. The last thing we need is another peacock strutting round the office.[21]

I want to give you a richer, more meaningful way to view your workplace and your current career trajectory.

From this perspective, the challenges you face at work are not simply annoying; they're crucial for your creative recovery. The dramas of day-to-day business aren't just a drag; they're essential for unleashing your creative potential. The often mind-numbing, soul-destroying, spirit-crushing reality of modern corporate life is, in fact, the precise platform to enable your full-blown creative transformation.

This is Carol Dweck's 'growth mindset' on acid.[22] This is when we change the game for good.

This is Zen, with a dash of Mr Squiggle and a whole lot of characters from *The Wizard of Oz*: seeing the hero's story in your career story, you can be at peace with where you are, wherever you are (Zen). Because you can re-create and reinvent whatever gets thrown your way (Mr Squiggle). And no matter what, you'll make it back to Kansas (Dorothy), because you'll find help along the way. And those who believe in and join you on your creative quest will wind up having their own creative transformation (Scarecrow, Tin Man and the Cowardly Lion).

---

[21] The key is to see yourself as an unanointed hero starting out on their quest, not the big shot returning home after finding success.

[22] If you're unfamiliar with Dweck's concept of a growth mindset, in her words, 'In a fixed mindset, people believe their basic qualities, like their intelligence or talent, are simply fixed traits', whereas 'In a growth mindset, people believe that their most basic abilities can be developed through dedication and hard work'. According to Dweck, a growth mindset 'creates a love of learning and a resilience that is essential for great accomplishment'.

TIME TO PLAY
Your Perfect Average Day

The point of this book is to reclaim your creativity so you can make more magic at work. A critical element in this process is to reimagine what work could look and feel like. Without a bold, brilliant, beautiful vision, there's nothing motivating you to do the work necessary to create it.

Which is why I'm now going to ask you to do an exercise I call **Perfect Average Day**.

Find a cosy corner, preferably outside or near a window. Make yourself a cup of tea, take out your favourite pen and your Everyday Creative journal and give yourself a good hour to sink into a sacred space of self-indulgence.

You're going to dream and design your **Perfect Average Day** one year in the future (or you could choose five or 10 years, whatever suits).

PERFECT meaning *perfect*. It could not have gone better. Every moment, from when you wake up until you fall asleep, is awesome. Whatever 'awesome' means to you. Let yourself lift the lid, no limitations, no boundaries. Dream big, in vibrant colour, and enjoy it.

AVERAGE meaning just a regular ol' Tuesday. There is nothing out of the ordinary, no significant events. You don't win the lottery or get a surprise promotion. It's a normal, run-of-the-mill day. But it's PERFECT.

When you write, be descriptive and visceral. Go into detail about your surroundings and how they make you feel.

You could write about waking up ...

Describe your bedroom, how it feels, what it looks like, smells like, sounds like. Is anyone with you? What happens when your feet hit the floor? Is it carpet, or timber, or polished concrete? What do you do in those first few moments? How do you feel? Where are you? What do you eat for breakfast? Do you eat breakfast? What time is it? What are you wearing? How do you feel about yourself, about the day ahead, about your life? How do you get to work? What do you think about on the way? Where are you working? What happens when you first walk in? Who do you see? How do they make you feel? How do you make them feel? (And on and on until you fall asleep.)

We grossly underestimate how much we limit our potential. If we can't imagine a bigger possibility for our lives, we won't believe it, and we certainly won't achieve it.[23]

I've done this exercise with executive teams across multiple industries and the results are always astounding. Especially with people who on paper 'don't have time for such a silly little activity'.

Participants often share what a revelation it is to stop and deeply consider how they want their day-to-day work experience to feel. To shift their focus from ticking boxes and delivering outcomes to reimagining the small moments that make them feel alive.

To be clear, this exercise is not about goal-setting or life planning.[24]

---

[23] I know how unbelievably lame that sounds—1980s motivational speaker much? Just go with it.

[24] And if you're thinking, 'But I'm perfectly happy with my life right now. I have everything I want. There's nothing I'd like to improve', close the book and give it to someone else. It's been nice hanging out but there are better things you could be doing with your time.

It is about:

1. **flexing your imagination**. Rebooting your internal dream machine. Until you have a vision for a creative, dynamic and enjoyable workplace, you'll never find ways to bring it to fruition. Einstein said, 'imagination is more powerful than knowledge'. This is why Olympic athletes spend so much time envisioning their performance. They're imprinting a potential and preferable reality into their subconscious. Which gives their subconscious a map full of cues to look out for while on the way to creating it.

2. **drawing out your deepest desires and authentic aspirations**. The frantic pace of modern life leaves us skimming the surface a lot of the time. When we dip into the depths of our subconscious it's often surprising and delightful what emerges through writing. Especially when writing through the senses.

3. **confronting your sense of self-worth**. This is a process to determine how valuable you deem yourself to be. Your desires are unconsciously influenced by what you believe you deserve. If you find yourself editing, censoring or diluting your idea of your perfect average day, and justifying the downgraded dream as being more reasonable and achievable, it is a sign of how limiting your belief-set is. If you find it difficult to dream big during this exercise, when it's just you and your journal, consider how much you're probably accepting less-than-favourable conditions in other areas of your life.

BONUS POINTS

The real power of a Perfect Average Day comes when you share it with your colleagues. If you run this as a group activity and take turns hearing from one another once you're done, you'll learn more about the people you work with (what their authentic interests are and what really matters to them) in an hour than you would in months or sometimes years.

This deepening awareness of the people you work with builds a rich connectedness across teams. But it also gives everyone a new set of meaningful data about one another. You find out what everyone wants from their work and their life. What's important to them. Why they've chosen to work at your company or in your industry.

And the best part is, when you articulate your Perfect Average Day for your colleagues, you're essentially sharing the responsibility for creating it. When the people you work with know what drives you, they become co-conspirators in the fulfilment of your aspirations. When you become aware of what they want (in work and life) you become an asset to them in helping them achieve it.

You're no longer solely responsible for engineering your ideal work experience. You've got a tribe of workplace warriors, all proactively cultivating an atmosphere that moves, inspires and nourishes your deepest desires. You've all multiplied the possibility of co-creating a workplace that, even on the most average of days, is breathtakingly perfect.

CHAPTER THREE

A Radical Rebirth

Declare your intent, *define your value*

Somewhere in the back half of 2012, I had the opportunity to buy a 99-year lease on a deserted island in the Gulf of Thailand. (Seriously.) I was living in Cambodia at the time, running a beach bar, guesthouse and Mexican restaurant, while debating whether to return home to Australia. It was one of those 'sliding doors' moments. Presented with this crazy opportunity, I had to think: Do I go deeper into this bizarre beach-filled life? Get dreadlocks and never wear shoes or a shirt again? Or do I return home, and attempt to find and fulfil my potential back in the big smoke?

I chose the latter, and in early 2014 I found myself in Melbourne starting my life again, *again*. After I did a few gigs, and was feeling moderately unfulfilled, a friend sent me a job description for a role as the community manager for a co-working community.

It sounded interesting. Two floors of start-ups. Lots of hungry, funky people working on dreams to make a difference. Beans bags, ping pong table and plenty of craft beer. Could *this* be the perfect platform for me to explore a new career path beyond performing music or owning a bar?

The trouble was, this would be my first adventure into a more 'traditional' work environment.[25] I'd never written a résumé before. I'd never had to go through a standard interview process. And my 'previous experience' was far from conventional as you could get.

But I wanted it. And I could see that I was perfect for the role. The challenge was getting my future employer to see it too.

So what did I do? I did what any Everyday Creative would do. *I got creative.* I leveraged the skills I already had and repurposed the experiences I'd already lived to carve out a place for myself where I had no place being.

I researched the community, familiarised myself with the vibe and read between the lines of who they were and wanted to be. Then I wrote a spoken-word piece that outlined my perception of their vision and the unique value I'd bring to help them fulfil it.

I then composed an original piece of music, inserted that and the poem I wrote over a video of me kayaking in Thailand, and boom! There's your résumé! When do I start?

Suffice to say, I got the job. The video (which you can find at www.everydaycreatives.com) went viral around the office and in the months (and years) following, I have spoken to many people who said that watching the video transformed the way they approached their own résumé.

The point of this story is not to write a poem as a cover letter for your next role (although I thoroughly recommend it and think the value of doing so will position you head and shoulders above the other applicants).[26] It's to recognise that your value in the emerging world

---

[25] Granted, I still rarely wore shoes, played an awful lot of Whitney Houston louder than people liked and threw an endless array of parties. But it could still be classed as a job. I *think*.

[26] The opportunity here is massive. Especially when so many companies are hiring for creativity and cultural fit. The riskiest thing you can do is play it safe, sending in a generic Word doc that gets lost in the hundreds of other digital documents. Very few people put in the effort to create a résumé that captures the essence of who they are. Or articulates the value they can bring to the organisation. Ask yourself: If you had to choose between two applicants, one who submitted a Word doc with a generic, impersonal-sounding cover letter, and the other, who dropped off a wooden box filled with personal artefacts that represent who they are, what's important to them and why they feel like they'd be an invaluable asset to your business... Who would you hire?

of work is not defined by what's on the job description. It's defined by what you can make of the experiences you've had in your life.

And it's becoming less about where you used to work (companies and brands) and more about what you've made with the world (a portfolio of projects that changed something).

If you want to stand out, if you want to be given more projects or positions that inspire and enliven you, you have to be proactive in demonstrating what is rare and radical about you.

Which means you've got to identify, nurture and liberate what is rare and radical about you!

And to do that, you've got to recognise that you already have skills, talents, expertise and experience that set you apart from your colleagues or other candidates. I'm not talking about certificates and accreditations. I mean the unique mindsets, skillsets and behaviours you've developed by living the life you've already lived.

Everyday Creatives are so effective in the workplace because they're each drawing on a bank of distinct, idiosyncratic experiences that no-one else has. They're leveraging a unique array of expertise that no-one else has access to. They are 100 per cent original in the way they show up and add value to the world around them.

This is what makes them so indispensable to their company, colleagues and clients. They have a way of dealing with challenges and finding opportunities that is entirely unique. And, as work changes and the talent pool grows, ensuring your value and relevance in the eyes of your company or clients has never been so important.

So what's the best approach for finding and defining your uniqueness?

You've got to be original

As William C. Taylor, author of *Simply Brilliant* and a respected global leadership adviser said, 'Stop trying to be the best, strive to be the only'. It's not enough to be the best anymore.

The Best

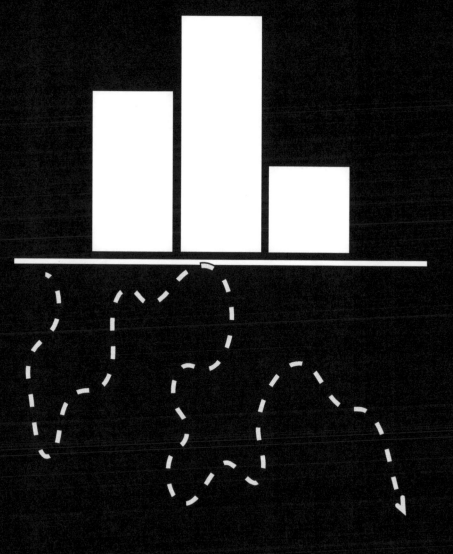

The Only

You've got to be a prototype. One of a kind. The most successful people are no longer the ones who do the same things faster, better or cheaper. They're the ones who champion the most original ideas, deliver out-of-the-box projects that are dripping with personality and do more of the things other employees can't (or won't).

Being original puts you in a league of your own and acts like a magnet to opportunity. You are without competition, unable to be replicated or replaced. It's the magic that turns heads, gets you noticed and keeps you front of mind.

And this desire for originality is on the rise in the workplace, as shown in chapter 2. Organisations now recognise that the people who have the most impact are the people who are brave enough to infuse their own style and flair into their work.

And the benefits of being an original extend far beyond how you're perceived or positioned in the workplace.

When you know who you are, what you stand for, what you love and what you're good at, you are exponentially more powerful.

Your passion is palpable. You're more intrinsically motivated. You can easily find a fifth gear when times get tough. You're more agile and resilient in the face of change. More innovative and imaginative in the face of challenges. You're accessing your full potential and operating from your full power.

But originality seems so elusive and unattainable. Reserved for those naturally cool types who were born to be badass. 'Can't I just be creative?' you might be wondering. 'Do I really have to be original too?'

Yes. Yes, you do.

'But how, Myke? What's the secret?'

Originality is intentional

What most people don't tell you about originality is that it's *intentional*.

Creative people, creative careers and creative lives don't happen by accident. They are designed. It's all too easy to be seduced by the idea that a unique talent or approach was bestowed upon someone at birth. That they've been blessed with more or better opportunities than you. That their success was written in the stars.

The reality is much less romantic but way more radical (and achievable).

The highly original folks who inspire you at work, in life or on Instagram have a secret. At some point they made a conscious decision to shape their identity and their environment to serve their self-expression. Their career and lifestyle are the direct result of a clear intent, a bold aspiration and a tremendous amount of action (aligned with their intent and aspiration).

They might not be overt about it. They might not even admit to it. But I promise you, they figured out what they love, what they want and what they're good at. Then doubled down on all three.

Don't be fooled whenever you hear someone say, 'We were just trying to write songs that felt meaningful to us. We really had no concern for whether the world would like them or not. So to receive this award for selling 10 million albums is really a surprise to us.'

I love their commitment to artistic integrity, but I call bullshit. Maybe they didn't expect to sell 10 million, but they definitely had a desire to be successful. And why wouldn't they? When did it become a crime to want more from your life and career? What's wrong with aspiring to have massive impact and reach?

Finding your originality

You may be thinking, 'Oh you make it sound so easy, Myke, but I'm different. I know I'm unique, but not in the ways that really matter. And certainly not in ways that help me at work. I'm not charismatic enough, gregarious enough, artistic enough, dangerous enough ...'

Stay with me. If you know there's something unique about you but you have a hard time distinguishing what it is, you're not alone. Most of us have never done the work to really define what sets us apart from our competitors.

In my experience, the biggest barriers to originality are a lack of:

≈ clarity

≈ confidence

≈ congruence.

What we misunderstand about originality is that discovering what's unique about you is a process of reflection and invention.

Clarity comes from noticing what comes naturally to you *and* deciding what you want to be known for. It's about embracing what lights you up *and* declaring the difference you're here to make.

If you haven't defined what's rare and radical about you, how will you ever know what to double down on? If you're unsure of what your superpower is, it's completely natural you'd lack the confidence to take more risks and rely on it.

Without the clarity of knowing who you are, and the confidence to be who you are, it's all too easy to lack congruence and become a mishmash of everyone else. To approach your work in different ways on different days. To get pulled and pushed around by the environment and never produce anything that you're either inspired by or proud of.

Becoming original is a creative act.

It's a conscious choice to decipher and curate what's important to you, then act in alignment with your choices. It's an ongoing experiment that fuses your vision and your self-expression. So the way we find yours is not to find it at all. It's to create it.

Think back on all the jobs you've had, all the life experiences you've had, all the significant relationships or 'sliding door' moments. See if you can find any recurring threads. What themes keep showing up in different situations or circumstances? What are the patterns that shape the seasons of your life?

What are the skills you developed, lessons you learned, and traits you took on from them? What meaning did you give your experiences? These are your most precious assets in the new world. The source of your originality and your enduring competitive advantage.

What can you take from the wild adventure you've already lived, and repurpose in your current job?

To the lighthouse

Adam Morgan is a brand strategist, respected author and founder of the global marketing agency EatBigFish. He was the first guy to coin the term 'challenger brand' when describing brands in a market that challenge and win against companies that are more recognisable and better resourced. More specifically, Morgan defined them as having a 'lighthouse identity': their sense of self is so strong, you notice them even when you're not looking for them (like a lighthouse).

Given that a lot of the work you'll do as an Everyday Creative mirrors that of a lighthouse brand, in that you're driven by vision and values but often lack the recognition or resources, it's helpful to apply the same lens to yourself as an individual.

Let's briefly explore the core elements of a lighthouse brand before we begin to articulate your own. As Morgan defined it, lighthouse brands have:

≈ **a strong point of view**. 'They have a distinct take on the world and every move they make tells us where they stand.'

≈ **a vivid intensity**. 'They offer an intense projection of who they are in everything they do.'

≈ **uncompromising salience**. 'They are highly intrusive, one cannot avoid noticing their activity even if not actively looking in their direction.'

≈ **a unique stance**. 'They assert a compelling conviction that the stance they are taking is one that is uniquely theirs.'

This richly defined value proposition separates challenger brands from the incumbents in their field. Every time you encounter them, however you encounter them, it's easy to understand how they see the world, what they care about and why they believe their point of view matters.

What kind of impact could you have if you (as an individual or your team) were positioned within your company as a lighthouse brand? Reflect on these questions to start defining it:

≈ Do you have a clear point of view? Are you clear on how you see the world, what matters to you and why you do what you do? Are you driven by a deep desire that is distinctly yours?

≈ Is your approach vivid and vibrant? With an intense projection of who you are in everything you do? Are you embedding your distinct personality into all aspects of your daily decisions?

≈ Are you prominent in all that you do? Not in an egotistical, attention-grabbing way, but is what you do and the way you do it so salient that people can't miss it, are drawn to it and can't stop talking about it?

≈ And is your stance uniquely your own? Do you walk your talk? Is there a legitimacy and credibility to what you do because your actions match your intentions? Is your professional brand built on rock?

A robotic reminder

So why am I harping on about being original? About identifying and defining your unique value and being so clear on your distinction that you start being seen as a lighthouse brand?

Aside from an increasingly competitive job market, don't forget what we covered in chapter 2. In the next few years, anything on your task list that can be automated will be automated. Many of the reasons you were initially employed in your current role will cease to exist.

You're going to have to prove your worth all over again. Day in, day out. Your value in the emerging economic climate does not depend on your capacity to do the work as it's designed: it depends on your ability to reinvent the work in ways no-one had dreamed.

It's no use trying to compete with a computer at what a computer does best. They will always beat you at chess, find a cheap carpark faster and reliably remind you when to eat your macros. But when it comes to anything complex or creative, emotional or relational, imaginative or artistic, you've got it licked.

It makes sense, then, that you shift your focus from being the best at what a computer can do, to being the best at everything a computer can't. And, while you're at it, shift your focus from being the *best* in relation to your colleagues and clients to being the *only*.

TIME TO PLAY
Your Personal Value Proposition

If companies were honest about the work required from their people these days, I reckon most job interviews would go something like this:

> So, we've put together a bunch of stuff in the job description that we think needs doing. There's some routine work that will probably get eaten by an algorithm soon. And there's a bunch of vague statements alluding to our culture and the kind of character we think fits well here.
>
> But truthfully, we're not really sure what your job will consist of. There's so much change happening every day. And we can guarantee there will be so many mishaps, hiccups, and stuff-ups, we kinda just need you to be awesome at everything. Solving problems we've never seen before, creating value in ways we haven't thought of yet, making magic around the office like someone we didn't know we needed but will struggle to continue without.
>
> So, can you just communicate to us what's rare and radical about you, and how you think you'll rock'n'roll this gig? And if we all feel it, you're in!

I don't want you to have to wait for that interview. Nor do I want you to be on the back foot when this kind of thing moves from the periphery to the centre. I want you to get the jump on the next decade and proactively position yourself as someone who matters.

And to do that, we're going to take your current job description and turn it into a value proposition. This is another opportunity for you to get creative while redefining your creative value.

At the start of this chapter I spoke about getting a job as a community manager for a co-working space upon returning from Cambodia. I had no prior experience but leveraged my unique skills and experience to give me an edge and get me the job (by making a video for a résumé).

Well, after a few months on the job, I realised that the real value I was bringing to the community extended far beyond what was written on my job description. So I decided to rewrite it.

I shared it with my boss, changed the job title in my email footer and set in motion a course of events that brought me to this moment right here. Such is the power of consciously and proactively articulating your value to the world (and your work).

Here is the value proposition for 'The Cultural Architect' (which was what I called myself).

The Cultural Architect

Reporting directly to the CEO, the Cultural Architect is responsible for exploring, understanding and articulating the unseen elements of our workplace culture.

They design and deploy evolving physical, mental and emotional spaces for our people to show up as the fullest expression of themselves.

The Cultural Architect crafts meaningful experiences through spontaneous moments of play that realign our people to their passion and our company to our cause.

They possess high levels of empathy and intuition. Have vast previous experience as an optimist and social artist. And is someone who is masterful at not only connecting to our people but connecting our people to each other.

The Cultural Architect is a gypsy, seeker, healer, lover, dreamer and believer who lives the stories they tell and tells stories that inspire others to live.

And has repeatedly shown the courage to love despite countless broken hearts.

This affords them a distinct advantage.

The Cultural Architect is the very beat of the heart of our company. They are the custodian of our collective potential and the caretaker of our conscious intent.

They act less like a navigator and more like a compass. They don't determine the businesses decisions; they merely remind us of who we are, where we've come from and where we hope to go.

They are the keeper of our deepest desires and serve as a safe place for us to reboot, replenish and reorganise our core priorities.[27]

---

[27] You can check out the full value proposition at everydaycreatives.com/resources

NOW IT'S TIME TO WRITE YOURS

Use this example as inspiration but make your Personal Value Proposition your own. Put your own flavour in it. Give yourself a new job title. New priorities and deliverables. Define the value that you're already bringing to your work that you're not currently (or officially) being measured on.

This differs from your creative manifesto in that it's specific to your current role, unique skills and experience. Look at what you're currently employed to do, then reflect on all the things you really do that make a difference at work: all the things that aren't on your job description but you're doing anyway. And in reality that's the highest value you add to your organisation.

This is your special sauce. This is your authentic edge. This is your gateway to Everyday Creativity. Define what is rare and radical about you. Infuse your personality into the document and bring it alive.

BONUS POINTS

If you want to take this to the next level (and of course you do), book a meeting with your boss. Tell them it's important to give it some gravitas. Then, armed with your new Personal Value Proposition, sit down opposite their desk and resign.

Pause for effect. Let them sit in it for a few moments. Then ask to be rehired in the role you've outlined in your Personal Value Proposition. Of course, you'll still be responsible for all the previous tasks, responsibilities and outcomes, but this is your opportunity to redefine your value in the eyes of those you work with (starting with your boss).

The added benefit of this is you're also setting up a structure of accountability. By sharing and declaring who you are, what your unique value is and what you want to be known for, you're giving your colleagues the clarity to help keep you on your path. They become wilful collaborators in your continuing self-development.

And if you're thinking, 'There's no way my boss would go for that', or 'I'd get laughed off the premises', there's even more reason for you to reimagine your résumé, redesign your value proposition and get the hell out of there!

Your Value Proposition

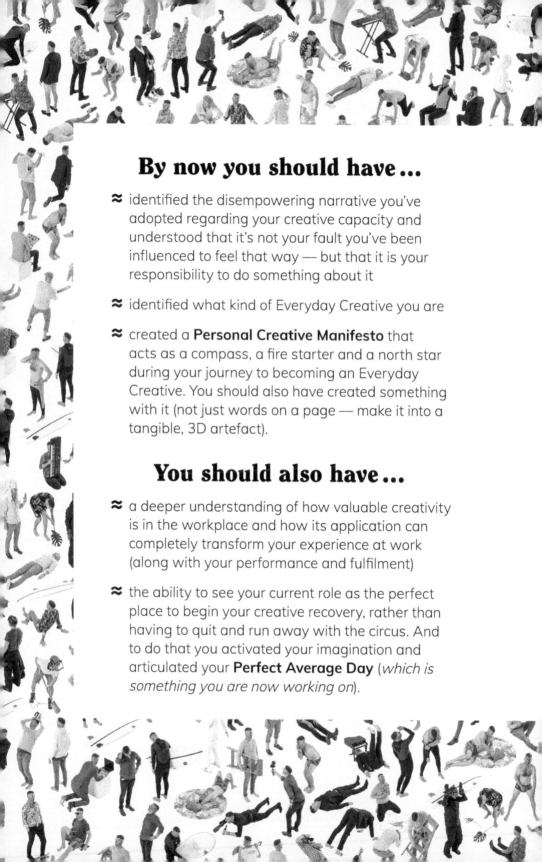

By now you should have...

≈ identified the disempowering narrative you've adopted regarding your creative capacity and understood that it's not your fault you've been influenced to feel that way — but that it is your responsibility to do something about it

≈ identified what kind of Everyday Creative you are

≈ created a **Personal Creative Manifesto** that acts as a compass, a fire starter and a north star during your journey to becoming an Everyday Creative. You should also have created something with it (not just words on a page — make it into a tangible, 3D artefact).

You should also have...

≈ a deeper understanding of how valuable creativity is in the workplace and how its application can completely transform your experience at work (along with your performance and fulfilment)

≈ the ability to see your current role as the perfect place to begin your creative recovery, rather than having to quit and run away with the circus. And to do that you activated your imagination and articulated your **Perfect Average Day** (*which is something you are now working on*).

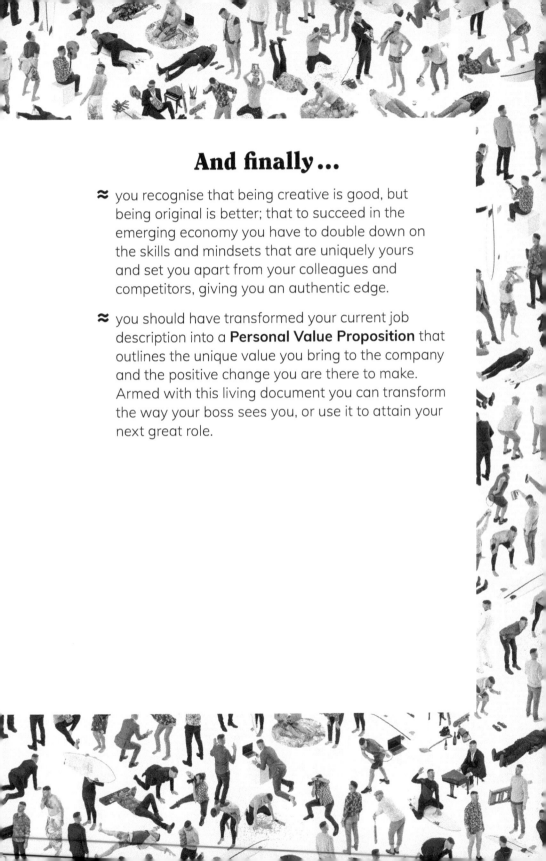

And finally...

≈ you recognise that being creative is good, but being original is better; that to succeed in the emerging economy you have to double down on the skills and mindsets that are uniquely yours and set you apart from your colleagues and competitors, giving you an authentic edge.

≈ you should have transformed your current job description into a **Personal Value Proposition** that outlines the unique value you bring to the company and the positive change you are there to make. Armed with this living document you can transform the way your boss sees you, or use it to attain your next great role.

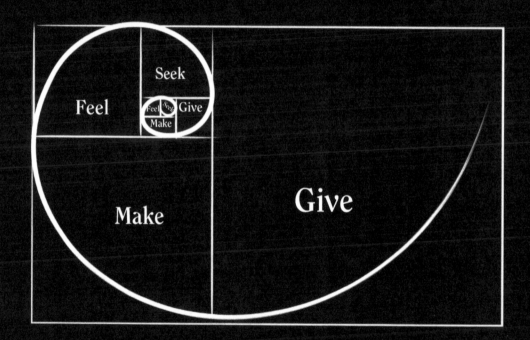

PART TWO

Developing The Practice

Now that you've:

≈ reclaimed your creative identity

≈ reimagined how your work can feel

≈ redefined your unique value

it's time to build your own creative practice.

There are four essential qualities that enable the work of an Everyday Creative. When practised in harmony they form a virtuous circle of creativity, compounding the impact you can have over time.

In part II, you'll explore each of these practices and discover simple, practical ways to apply them immediately at work and in your life.

Remember that creativity isn't a gift or talent; it's a muscle and a habit. The more you use it, the more you have.

CHAPTER FOUR

The Courage To Seek

Rekindle a *sense of wonder*

Most people book a holiday based on the brochure. They prearrange their airport transfers. Reserve a hotel massage. Curate a list of the best restaurants (as voted by Google). They'll post photos of popular landmarks and jump on organised tours, unconsciously seeking the familiar in the unknown. *We call them tourists.*

There are others, however, who revel in the uncertainty of new experiences. They eat where the locals eat. Adapt their plans according to how each day unfolds. They feel quite at home without a map or a compass. They're more likely to buy one-way tickets, venture off the beaten path and be guided by the rhythmical dance of choice and chance. *We call them travellers.*

Everyday creatives are travellers, not tourists.

They view their work as a pilgrimage. A sacred quest of self-discovery. They don't come for the hype or the highlight reel. They see the hiccups, mishaps and setbacks of the road as central to their reason for travelling it.

And this restless desire to go further, listen deeper and stay longer gives them an uncanny ability to transform and transcend whatever circumstances they might encounter along the way.

From contempt to curiosity

To become an Everyday Creative you don't have to quit your job, sell all your possessions and book a one-way ticket to the other side of the world. You do have to summon and leverage the same restless curiosity a traveller uses to begin and sustain their journey. But apply it, instead, to the trials and tribulations of your everyday work.

When I speak about finding the courage to seek, it's about:

≈ harnessing the agitation you feel after walking out of another pointless meeting

≈ channelling the irritation you experience when faced with the snail's pace of your company

≈ leveraging the disappointment of watching your work be compromised yet again.

An Everyday Creative uses curiosity and contempt in equal measure. They marinate their frustration in fascination. They seek the seeds of new ideas in the daily annoyances they feel in their job. They recognise that...

frustration is fuel.

When you embrace the dissatisfaction you feel at work, and use curiosity to transcend your contempt, you'll realise that most of the rules, systems and processes that confine you are not immovable objects or natural laws; they were just someone else's idea. Something that worked once or was agreed upon way back when. Something that can just as easily be challenged, adjusted or evolved.

This perspective is the driving force behind every product innovation, brand decision and strategic mission.

Unlike creativity, at least in a business context, curiosity isn't just about solving problems. It's about exploration and expansion. Curiosity can start and lead us anywhere. And that's exactly the kind of mindset we need in business. But equally, it's what scares the life out of many organisations and leaders—unless, of course, you're someone like Michael Houseman.

Firefox vs Safari

In 2013, Michael Houseman, the chief analytics officer at Cornerstone, led a project to find out why some customer service employees stayed in their jobs longer than others. His team collated data from over 30 000 employees across multiple industries in the United States.

Following a hunch, he decided to test whether there was any correlation between an employee's choice of internet browser and the length of their tenure.

Surprisingly, the employees who used Firefox or Chrome to browse the web stayed at their jobs 15 per cent longer than those who used Internet Explorer or Safari. Even more surprising was that the pattern was the same for absenteeism: Firefox and Chrome users were 19 per cent less likely to miss work.

But the real kicker came when the researchers measured performance. Using over three million data points on sales, customers satisfaction and average call length, they found that the Firefox and Chrome users sold more stuff, in less time and had happier customers than their peers.

After probing deeper into the data they came to realise the results had nothing to do with the browsers themselves. The four groups, on average, had similar typing speed and technical knowledge of a computer. What mattered was how they came to use their preferred browser.

Internet Explorer[28] and Safari are the built-in browsers for their operating systems. If you used Firefox or Chrome you had to look beyond the default option you were given. You had to use your initiative to find an alternative browser, then make the effort to download and install it in your own time.

---

[28] For the progressives out there, Internet Explorer is now called Microsoft Edge. Whatever that means.

This tiny difference in behaviour pointed to a powerful difference in character. And a significant difference in performance.

The employees who changed their browser rarely stuck to the script. They put more personality into each call and responded with more curiosity and creativity to any and all challenges within the role.

Those who accepted the default browsers, however, rarely strayed from the standard operating procedure. They saw their job as fixed, had a hard time adapting to unforeseen situations and inevitably became burnt out by the rigid and repetitive nature of the work.

Now, I'm not saying that if you change your browser you'll become an instant creative genius. But if you're someone who has a healthy distaste for the default, you're far more likely to find opportunities to express your creativity at work. And, judging by the research, you're far more likely to perform better too.

The first step in finding the courage to seek is to develop a healthy distaste for the default.

Surrender the script

In 2009, I worked as a call centre operator for a social research firm. The place was full of musicians and actors trying to subsidise their artistic endeavours. We had a quota of completed interviews to hit every day. And it was imperative we followed the script.

I never followed the script. And for good reason: it was terrible. Whenever I did I'd get hung up on or receive a tirade of abuse. So I did it my way, and, as boring and repetitive as that job was, I loved it.

I never knew who would pick up, where they were in the country, or how the call would unfold. My imagination would run wild with the sound of their voice or the noise in the background. And the challenge of building rapport in seconds to influence a complete stranger to do a 45-minute interview was fricken radical.

Much to the dismay of my superiors, who would reprimand me every few days or threaten to fire me if I didn't do it like I was told, I kicked arse. I consistently outperformed my peers, was moved on to more challenging projects and then hilariously won 'interviewer of the year' at the Christmas party (which was judged by numbers, not by the nature of the interview). And all because I found a way to be curious with the work.

Curiosity isn't just the gateway to more creativity, it's the source of your competitive advantage.

Making work work for you

Think about your current work. In fact, let's go one step further. Think about the shittiest parts of your job. The most repetitive, pointless or bureaucratic. Something you just can't deal with, and even the thought of it makes you sigh.

Got it? Now answer me this. How can you infuse more of your personality into that specific task? How can you step over what's expected, look beyond your boss or best practice and do it in a way that works for you? However novel, impractical or unconventional?

I'm sure you have plenty of reasons for why that particular thing can't be done any other way. But I challenge you to consider how it can. This is precisely why and where you want to flex your curiosity and put the game back on your terms. Use it to make your experience at work better.

I promise you there are an infinite number of alternatives hidden in plain sight. The barriers to more creativity in your work are less about coming up with new ideas and more about finding the courage to act on them.

I've give you an example. Hands up if you love email! Anyone...

Anyone...

Well, I do. It's one of my favourite things. Here's why.

I centre-align my emails

Seriously.

I've been doing it for years.

And it's been a revelation.

I used to hate email.

The layout was uninspiring.

Its vibe so beige and impersonal.

Until one uneventful day,

while procrastinating over an email,

I got curious about the platform.

Started moving my mouse,

clicking on a few things,

until I discovered

the centre-align button.

It reminded me of all the years

I spent writing poetry and songs.

In those days I'd always centre-align

because I liked the way it looked.

Enjoyed the way it felt.

And loved the way it

changed the way I wrote.

I'd phrase things differently

because I was conscious of

the shape of the text.

I'd lean heavy into rhyme

and alliteration for effect.

Writing emails became a joyful activity

to express my wildest creativity.

And the impact stretched well beyond

my personal satisfaction.

It became a canary in a coal mine.

A way to curate my clients.

When I get a reply from a senior exec

who has taken the time

to right-align their text,

to use coloured headings

and mismatched fonts,

there's a very high probability

we'd end up working together.

And that work will be delightfully

creative right from the outset.

But even more than that,

it now acts as a trigger for

solidifying my identity.

Every time I centre-align,

I'm reminded of my choice to be creative.

It reaffirms for me that I'm a risk-taker,

rule-breaker and mischief-maker.

Which, in turn, empowers me

to stay curious, stay courageous

and keep creating.

All of this magic

from just one click.

Born to seek

Fortunately, we are all hardwired for wonder: biologically designed to reflect, ruminate and reimagine the world around us. And this innate capacity to ask questions serves more than merely an evolutionary purpose.

Neuroscientists have identified a part of the brain they call 'the seeking system': a neural network that runs between the prefrontal cortex and the ventral striatum. When our seeking system is activated, blood rushes to the brain, dopamine is released and we are filled with positive feelings of awe, wonder and the search for meaning.

This invigorated sense of anticipation results in what Martin Seligman, a psychologist at the University of Pennsylvania, calls 'zest'—a greater appreciation and enthusiasm for life. When we feel a sense of zest we experience life and work as a wild, untamed adventure. A puzzle to be played with; a mystery to be unravelled. We approach new situations and unexpected changes with enthusiasm and excitement instead of apprehension and anxiety.

Isn't that how you'd love to feel at work? Excited and enthusiastic, vibrant and alive? Passionately engaged in the tasks that lie before you?

Seeking—curiosity—quite simply makes our lives better, more colourful, dynamic, mysterious and enchanting. It propels us toward deeper engagement, improves intelligence and boosts physical and mental wellbeing. And if we wield it with consistency and conviction, it makes our careers more robust, rewarding and reliable.

So if curiosity is so essential to our lives, so effortless for our minds, and so desired by our organisations, why aren't we using it more? Why aren't our organisations encouraging and enabling curiosity? And why do so many of us find it so difficult to be curious at work?

Resistance to rumination

Generally speaking, the world has been at war with wonder for centuries. Our oldest stories about curiosity are warnings. Consider Adam and

Eve and the apple of knowledge, Icarus and the sun, Pandora's box. It was St Augustine who said 'God fashioned hell for the curious'. It was Buddha who told us 'to seek is to suffer'. And we all know what killed the cat.

As Ian Leslie, author of *Curious: The Desire to Know and Why Your Future Depends on It* explains, 'For most of Western history, curiosity has been regarded as at best a distraction, at worst a poison, corrosive to the soul and to society.'

This should come as no surprise. Curiosity poses a direct threat to the status quo. It is the genesis of change and the root of every revolution. Our impulse for inquiry is dangerous to those who want to keep things as they are. And let's be honest: most organisations are filled with people who want to keep things exactly as they are.

Despite the corporate rhetoric and impassioned executive pleas, most of my clients speak of their difficulty in bringing more curiosity to their company. This sentiment is echoed in research conducted by Harvard professor Francesca Gino, who found that only 24 per cent of us feel curious in our job, and around 70 per cent say we face significant barriers to asking more questions at work.

There seems to be a divide in our relationship with curiosity depending on where we sit in the hierarchy. In a study conducted by Survey Monkey in 2018, 83 per cent of C-suite execs said curiosity is encouraged 'a great deal' in their company, while only 52 per cent of their people agree. And a staggering 82 per cent of individuals are convinced that curiosity makes no difference to their compensation.

If you don't believe you're being paid to be curious, why would you be?

Take a moment now to reflect on your workplace:

≈ How comfortable are they, really, with curiosity?

≈ Are they open to any and all questions?

≈ Are they at ease when they don't have all the answers?

≈ Do they celebrate and encourage those who attempt to change things?

≈ Or do they punish those who ponder?

≈ Do they mock or make fun of those who put forward half-baked ideas?

≈ Do they suppress any attempts to try something new in favour of doing what we did last year?

If your workplace leaves something to be desired in the way of encouraging curiosity, you're not alone. Most organisations still see curiosity as a liability, not an asset. People who ask too many questions are seen as a disturbance or an inconvenience. Add to that the frenetic pace of the modern workplace and the increasing pressure to deliver, and it's all too easy to slip into predictable routines.

But there are deeper, more personal reasons for why we find it difficult to ask questions at work.

Curiosity requires humility.

To be curious is to accept that you don't have all the answers. You have to surrender your status or expertise in the hope of learning something new, and this is difficult for a lot of us. Especially at work.

By acknowledging we don't know something, there's a risk we'll be cast as incompetent, indecisive or unintelligent. It's better to keep up the pretence of being all-knowing than reveal any gaps in our knowledge or expertise.

And this mindset is exacerbated higher up the chain: the more we know, the less we think we have to learn. Business leaders start believing they're expected to have all the answers instead of asking more questions. This kind of thinking can unintentionally cultivate a culture that prioritises getting things done over doing things differently—even if it means doing things that are ineffective or inconsequential.

But the biggest barrier to curiosity is that, deep down, we're afraid of what we'll find.

By asking deeper questions about our people and processes, our company and career, we open ourselves up to uncomfortable truths.

What if our current job isn't just boring, it goes against our values? What if who we spend our time with at work is more about convenience than meaningful connection? What if our career path is less about producing work that matters and more about proving we matter to someone?

A SPARKLY COMPLAINT

Two years ago, a friend of mine (we'll call her Laura) landed a role as organisation development manager for a large manufacturing company with an 85-year legacy in Australia.

She was hired to shake up the space. To breathe new life into the culture and bring the business into the twenty-first century.

Naturally, she wore modern attire as opposed to a grey corporate suit. She liked to move around the office and work from a laptop instead of barricading herself behind a three-walled cubicle. And she was passionate and imperfect rather than reserved, compliant or agreeable when discussing the many possibilities for improving the employee experience.

Then one day, within a month of starting, she was called into the GM's office.

He told me there had been a formal complaint made about my shoes,[29] and to a degree my general presence. They were too loud for the office and some long-term employees.

(continued)

---

[29] Laura has a borderline obsession with a particular style of shoe by Adidas called the 'shell toe'. And the kind she wore at work that gained her this formal complaint was covered with glitter and sparkles.

A SPARKLY COMPLAINT (cont'd)

Seriously. A formal complaint made about my shoes.

And how did that make her feel?

Not great. That can really crush your soul (pardon the pun) when people see you for what you wear instead of what you bring to a business. Especially when that business was so obviously stuck in the eighties.

Fortunately, the MD was more progressive than his counterparts and pushed the complaint to one side. This was, however, the beginning of what felt like a targeted campaign titled, 'that's not how we do things around here'.

Over the next 12 months Laura's budgets were cut, her projects were put on hold and the possibilities she was promised were reduced or diluted at every turn.

Anyone would be forgiven for jumping ship at that point. But Laura stuck with it. She found the resources she needed in the most unlikely of places and went on to deliver a suite of successful capability-building programs that are having a radical impact on the business.

When I asked her how she managed to stay sane, focused and optimistic in spite of her detractors, she said,

The whole 'sparkly shoes' incident showed me loud and clear that this business wasn't going to be my inspiration for change. I knew I'd have to look elsewhere.

I'm highly visual so I spent my weekends going to art galleries and finding beautiful graphic design publications. I'd retreat to my fancy notebooks and expensive designer stationery, even for just a few minutes, to keep me motivated and inspired.

I'd even sneak a quick peek at my glittery white kicks during meetings to help me feel creative in an environment which clearly was not.

When creativity went AWOL for Laura at work, she went looking for it elsewhere. And by keeping herself inspired outside of work she managed to stay inspired inside of work. Despite the roadblocks and setbacks, she never compromised on her intention to make the world (and her company) more beautiful and creative.

Over time, the business began to change and the right people started to take notice. Two years on, 'culture' is now a pillar of the organisation's strategy and Laura was just named Head of People and Performance.

When I asked her how it feels to be a 33-year-old executive of a household name business, she replied,

I'm just excited about what this means for my work. Now I can start doing something really exciting. And the best part is, my shoes are even louder than before!

The real danger

The real danger of not asking the questions that matter is that we'll become nothing more than a passenger. Happy to wait in queues, follow the formula and accept the only options as the only options. This approach will never produce anything original, and the impact extends well beyond the workplace.

If you're not intentional about learning, brave enough to step outside your comfort zone and explore more of what is available to you, you risk more than the quiet atrophy of your creativity. Your life will become a patchwork quilt of reactionary choices.

You'll end up with work you're not proud of and a career you're not inspired by. You'll wake up one day and realise the circumstances of your life have largely been decided by someone else. That you've unconsciously accepted and compromised on everything that matters to you.

I'm not saying you should be entitled or ungrateful, always demanding more. I'm suggesting we could all be more focused and intentional about who we are and what we want to be.

This is the true power of seeking: not just to have more and better ideas, not just to feel alive and energised at work. But to become deeply aware of who you are, what matters to you and why you're here. To ask bigger, broader and more beautiful questions about the difference you want to make and the legacy you want to leave.

How to be more curious

Whoa. That just got kinda heavy. Let's bring it back to what you can do today. Here are a few ideas for returning to your curious roots...

Diversify your stimuli

When Mihaly Csikszentmihalyi, the eminent psychologist of creativity, was asked to describe how creative people differ from others he remarked, 'Complexity. They show tendencies of thought and action that in most people are segregated. They contain contradictory extremes; instead of being an "individual," each of them is a "multitude."'

Here's the truth. You're not going to find the answers you need to win at work, at work. At least not in your current role and routine. You've got to expose yourself to a wider palette of influence. Place yourself in a variety of unfamiliar situations, and immerse yourself in a diverse array of unique experiences.

If creativity is the art of connecting dots, then curiosity is the art of collecting them.

What does this look like? Go to events outside of your industry. Sit in on meetings outside of your department. Read articles, listen to podcasts and watch films about topics you have no understanding of. Stuff your brain with a delightfully diverse diet of interesting ideas. To rekindle your sense of wonder, you need to live a richer, more varied life.

The more diverse the inputs, the more distinct the outputs. You must cultivate a daily habit of finding and following what fascinates you. The most creative people I know read more books, watch more interesting films, go to new places and meet new people.

And for supercharged results, go for the edges. Be the traveller we talked about at the beginning of this chapter. Read the classics, not just shallow click-bait articles online. Go see live music, don't just listen to algorithmic playlists through your laptop speakers. Talk to strangers, talk to your customers, talk to your competitors. Resist the urge to gravitate toward familiar faces, places and routines.

Get hungry for the new, the novel and the next and both your curiosity and creativity will compound like interest.

Make room for space

Talk to any gym junkie about putting on muscle and they'll tell you rest days are just as important as the days you lift weights. That's when the muscle repairs, rebuilds and regenerates.

The same is true for your creativity. You can't just stuff your brain with new information and stay forever focused on the task at hand. You need to let your mind exhale. And not just for rest and rejuvenation.

Quick reminder ...

... to exhale

Taking breaks, letting ideas percolate or heading off on year-long sabbaticals are all well documented as crucial elements of the creative process. Heck, even taking a nap has been scientifically proven to help with creativity.[30] But taking a break is one of those things we tend to do hours, weeks or years after we should. It's often just a reaction to exhaustion or overwhelm. We do it once we've hit a wall or run out of ideas. And when we do, we prefer to just veg out, watch a little Netflix or nap. But that's missing the real potential of space.

Studies have shown that engaging in simple, low-cognitive tasks between times of focused attention leads to more creative ideas. Activities that are boring or routine enough to facilitate a wandering mind are vital for marinating and incubating our ideas. Daydreaming, despite being considered lazy and ineffective, is essential for innovation.

This is why we have so many great ideas in the shower. Or while walking, driving or cooking. There's enough going on to keep our conscious mind entertained, so our subconscious can get to work without being watched.

I quite like the way Jonah Lehrer put it in his essay 'The virtues of daydreaming' in *The New Yorker*: 'A daydream is just a means of eavesdropping on the novel thoughts generated by the unconscious.'

When you take a break before you need to and switch your attention to another activity that requires little cognitive processing, you give your subconscious the space and privacy it needs to reconfigure all the information you've collected in new, novel and unconventional ways.

Think about all those ping pong tables in common areas of newly renovated offices. I used to think they were a shallow attempt at 'building a creative culture'. It turns out, a little light ping pong in between brainstorming sessions might be a powerful recipe for creativity.

So what are some simple activities you could do at work to give your conscious mind a rest, while giving your subconscious the space it

---

[30] Dr Sara C. Mednick, an associate professor of psychology, found that 90 minutes of REM sleep does wonders for creative thinking and problem solving.

needs to make magic? And if you really want to kick it into fifth gear, make it something physical. Use your hands and move your body.

Kill your routine

Now, before you go scheduling every minute of your week with new experiences or naps, I'm going to suggest something that flies in the face of popular culture.

Kill your routine. At least occasionally. And always intentionally. Embrace Mark Twain's philosophy for life: 'Everything in moderation, including moderation.'

We have an unhealthy obsession with optimisation. So many of us are suffocating beneath the weight of morning routines, evening routines, creative routines, mindfulness routines. All in the name of better performance.

Routine, however, can be devastating to our curiosity. Because curiosity needs variety; it thrives on surprise and is delighted by disruption. As author Paulo Coelho said, 'If you think adventure is dangerous, try routine; it is lethal'.

There are endless lists of products, innovations, songs and stories that were the result of an unexpected accident, a serendipitous rendezvous, an unintended circumstance. These disruptions are gifts. They hold the secret to our creative salvation.

If you're not willing to seize those unexpected moments, to surrender control of your schedule and liberate yourself from the shackles of your routine, you'll miss the gift of providence.

I'm not saying you should sleep in, cancel your engagements and wander the streets until midnight. But give yourself permission to:

≈ lean in when life throws you a curly one

≈ stay in the magic when the magic arises

≈ squeeze every drop out of a serendipitous rendezvous that ignites your curiosity.

The gift of Vuja De

When you commit to becoming curious about your work—when you choose to use your dissatisfaction as a catalyst for creativity—you can find a way to make magic with anything. Especially the work you don't like.

When you develop the courage to seek you'll give yourself the best opportunity to experience what comedian George Carlin called 'Vuja De'.[31]

Vuja De is the opposite of Deja Vu. It happens when you enter a situation you've been in a thousand times before, but with the sense of being there for the first time. It's when we encounter the familiar but see it with fresh eyes.

As French novelist Marcel Proust said, 'The real act of discovery consists not in finding new lands but in seeing with new eyes'. And this is the work of an Everyday Creative. To relentlessly ask questions about why things are the way they are. And put forward new ideas about how they could be. To see everyday work as a playground of possibility.

---

[31] This phrase was explored in depth by author Bob Sutton in his 2001 book *Weird Ideas That Work*.

TIME TO PLAY

Choose one of these to action this week.

1. **Treat yo'self to wonder.** Attend one event outside of your industry, one meeting outside of your department and one experience completely unrelated to your work that makes you come alive. Listen intently, take notes, be the first to volunteer. Bonus points for raising your hand before you've even thought of a question.

2. **Schedule depression sessions.** Engineer all your meetings to include a 10-minute depression session at the end. Use that time to reflect and process what you just covered. Daydream by a window, take a stroll outside or engage in a low-cognitive task like juggling or doodling. Bonus points for inviting your fellow meeting attendees to join you or do the same.

3. **Accept one invitation you shouldn't.** Seize one opportunity to follow your fascination longer than you intended (or are allowed). Turn a chance encounter into a meaningful conversation over coffee. Expand a moment of insight into an hour of fully forming a new idea. Bonus points if you blow off the entire afternoon and end up at the pub.

4. **Establish a daily LIP.** Start and finish every workday with a 'Learning In Progress' meeting. By yourself or with your team ask, 'What is one topic or activity I am curious about today? What is one thing I often take for granted that I want to find out more about? What is one practice or process I would like to change and why?' Bonus points for breaking rules, threatening the status quo or barbecuing a sacred cow.

5. **Create a shrine of curiosities.** Find a corner in the office (or at your desk) and fill it with interesting ideas, artefacts and reflections. Put images up that inspire you and physical objects that evoke your imagination. It could be about a person or a process. It could be the result of a success or failure. Bonus points for commandeering an entire room for curiosity.

CHAPTER FIVE

The Courage To Feel

Activate your *social, emotional and aesthetic intelligence*

One of the greatest Australian films of all time took just five weeks to make, from idea to final edit. *The Castle* became an instant cult classic, grossing over $10 million at the box office and cementing its place within the Australian cultural landscape.

Set in the early 1990s, in an outer suburb of Melbourne, it tells the story of a working-class family (the Kerrigans) in a battle with big business. In a David and Goliath–style tale, the patriarch and lead protagonist, Darryl Kerrigan, fights his way to the Supreme Court to keep his family home from being bulldozed for a proposed airport development.

In one infamous scene, Darryl's small-time-lawyer friend, Dennis Denuto (played by Tiriel Mora), is making their case in the first of many court appearances. Struggling his way through much of his appeal, Denuto's closing statements have become the stuff of legend:

In summing up. It's the constitution. It's Mabo.
It's justice. It's law. It's ... it's the vibe.

I'm sure you've had moments like that at work. Struggling to express how you feel and why it matters. Fumbling and bumbling with the limits of language. Contorting your face, shrugging your shoulders, gesturing wildly with your hands, all in a failed attempt to articulate 'the vibe'.

That misunderstood magic that is so palpable yet so intangible. So obvious yet so easy to overlook. So meaningful and yet so hard to measure.

But as difficult as it is, and foolish as it sometimes feels, learning to decipher, define and design 'the vibe' is an essential skill for the modern workplace, and the secret weapon of an Everyday Creative. Why? Because...

Feeling is the new thinking

Like it or not, *believe it or not*, the new era of business is as much about feeling as it is about thinking. As much about 'the vibe' as an indicator of value as it is about data, metrics and analysis.

How you feel about yourself, your colleagues and clients, the work you do and the company you work for, greatly influences the quality, quantity and consistency of your output.

How your customers and colleagues feel about you defines the value, length and profitability of those relationships. Heck, the way you feel about this sentence, chapter and book will determine whether you choose to keep reading it, get value from it or share it.

How we feel affects what we buy and where we choose to work. It influences team performance and interpersonal relationships. It even shapes our identity and professional success.

IMHO, feeling is the most underrated aspect of business today. It makes your ideas more sticky, your relationships more meaningful, and the impact of your output more potent and long-lasting. And it's the second essential practice for an Everyday Creative.

Feeling is:

≈ the strongest driver of human behaviour

≈ the fastest way to build meaningful connections (between people, projects and products)

≈ the source of a business's competitive advantage.

But don't just take my word for it.

Experience is everything

Although we like to believe we're all rational, reasonable beings making logical, pragmatic choices, research tells us otherwise. Studies have shown that up to 95 per cent of our decisions are driven by our subconscious. And emotion, not reason, is the language of our subconscious mind.

Add to that the rise of the 'experience economy',[32] the proliferation of companies focusing on redefining their employee experience and the increasing demand for more emotional intelligence in the workplace, and the case for feeling begins to carry a whole lot more weight.

According to Expedia, a staggering 74 per cent of people are prioritising experiences over products when it comes to their spending habits. People young and old are opting out of accumulating more stuff and are instead investing their hard-earned cash into moments that become meaningful memories. And for good reason. Studies have shown that investing in experiences brings more long-lasting joy than spending money on things.

---

[32] A phrase first coined in 1998 by Joseph Pine and James Gilmore, the 'experience economy' is defined as an economy where consumers buy memorable events and the effects they have on an individual or group. Put so eloquently in their HBR article, 'a company intentionally uses services as the stage, and goods as props, to engage individual customers in a way that creates a memorable event'.

Look at some of the most iconic brands of the last decade. It's obvious how instrumental 'the experience' was in amplifying their success. From Apple to Nike to Tesla, they don't just invest in what a product does or what problem it solves. They focus intently on how it feels to use and how it feels to be seen to use it.

Although I had hoped to get through an entire book without using them as an example, look at Uber. They didn't just transform the transportation experience; they changed they way we experience time. While waiting for our ride, we can watch the little cartoon car snake its way through the side streets on a digital map. Even when my ride takes longer to arrive than a taxi, watching my driver snake their way through the suburbs is surprisingly satisfying.

Some companies have even built their entire business model on the power of experience. Secret Cinema have redefined the way we experience film by building life-sized replicas of the sets of critically acclaimed movies, complete with hundreds of actors as characters from each film. For hours before actually watching the film, patrons exist *in* the film.

Or then there is the UK company Black Tomato, who have an offering called 'Get Lost'. Starting at £22 000, clients work with a personalised consultant to determine what is missing from their life. Then, on a particular time on a particular day, they are whisked from their home to the airport, put on X number of flights, Y number of taxis and possibly a helicopter ride, then dropped in the Atacama Desert of North Chile, or on a glacier in the fjords of Iceland, or some other remote location, with a just a backpack, a GPS and the instruction 'We'll see you in a week'.

This appetite for experience doesn't stop with consumers. It has infiltrated what we now desire and demand from our work. Websites such as LinkedIn and Glassdoor make it easier for prospective employees to assess the atmosphere of a company they're considering.

No longer can companies hide behind sexy employer branding campaigns or rely on savvy recruiters to position themselves among recruits. They need to back it up, follow through and invest in a whole lot more than a ping pong table and a case of craft beer.[33]

Yup, it's a radical time to be in business. And for those brave enough to look deeper into feeling, emotion and experience, like us Everyday Creatives, the opportunities are unparalleled.

So if feeling is so essential to our lives and so impactful at work, why do we see so much resistance to it in the office?

---

[33] To today's increasingly woke employees, a lot of how a company feels is determined by what it stands for. A growing number of people want to work for a company that considers its social and environmental impact. A brand that isn't just interested in 'doing more good' through a shallow corporate social responsibility program but in 'doing less harm' and consciously redirecting their investments or re-engineering their supply chain to be more ethical and sustainable.

How does this make you feel?

Barriers to feeling

Let's be honest: to speak earnestly about 'feeling' in most boardrooms today would leave us open to ridicule and regret. Despite our best intentions for a more human-centric workplace—one that allows, encourages and champions the entire spectrum of the human emotion—we're not all there just yet.

We've been told for years to 'keep our feelings under control' or 'not get too carried away'. We've been undermined for 'being too emotional', shamed for 'oversharing', laughed at for sounding 'a bit touchy-feely'.

If we start harping on about the 'vibe' of our latest offering or the 'feel' of the next leadership offsite, we can so easily end up sounding fluffy and esoteric. Lightweight and inconsequential.

And when you consider how clinical and impersonal most workplaces are, is it any wonder we slip on a sanitised suit of amour when we step into the office? It should come as no surprise that we willingly dull our senses and distance ourselves from the emotional impact of our work.

All of this avoidance to feeling is underlined by a general consensus that feeling is too hard to measure, too difficult to control, too uncomfortable to articulate and too inconvenient to scale. And some of those concerns are somewhat legitimate.

Feeling is intangible, inconsistent and idiosyncratic. It won't always fit within a formula and rarely submits to a standardised system. And in a world that worships quantitative data and analysis it's no surprise we struggle to fit qualitative sensibilities into the spreadsheet.

The problem with our fixation on the figures is that the information we gather is almost always decontextualised. In order to measure something, we must reduce its totality to squeeze it into a simple set of numbers.

I'll give you an example. We can count the number of people in a room, make a pie chart to illustrate the gender balance and build a 3D model of who sits next to whom. But all that data tells us nothing of the atmosphere of the room or the quality of interactions between people.

Is it upbeat or flat? Optimistic or cynical? Euphoric or melancholy?

If you're looking to motivate, influence or inspire, which do you think is more effective: showing them stats or sharing a story? Demanding they think differently or making them feel deeply?

As education scholar Elliot Eisner pointed out, 'Not all that matters can be measured, and not everything that can be measured, matters'.

Feeling can be hard to work with, but work with it we must. Because despite the perks or the pay packet, we work harder and smarter when we feel something. And our customers stay longer, engage more deeply and share louder when they feel something.

And putting more feeling in our work doesn't require vast amounts of time and resources. It could be as simple as a well-placed question. No more than seven simple words. Like what Shane McCurry did with his voicemail.

SORRY I MISSED YOUR CALL...

In 2019, while attending a conference in Byron Bay, I met a beautiful guy named Shane McCurry. Shane is a high-performance leadership adviser, with a long list of successful companies and elite sporting teams as clients.

A few months after our meeting, I missed a call from Mr McCurry about doing a little work together. When I returned his call, I missed him and was diverted to his voicemail message.

I was expecting a pretty standard kind of message, like 'Hi it's Shane, sorry I missed you. If you could leave your name and number' et cetera. And most of it was just like that. Until he finished with an invitation that stopped me in my tracks.

'... and if you feel like it, tell me one thing you're grateful for.'

I was floored. A hundred different things came rushing to my mind. An ocean of memories and relationships. I'll admit there was a good 10 seconds of radio silence as I paused and got present to all I was grateful for in my life.

(continued)

SORRY I MISSED YOUR CALL... (cont'd)

Aside from being such a beautiful way to disrupt my day, what struck me most about Shane's invitation was how quickly it altered my emotional state. How it happened so effortlessly and in the most unlikely of places.

When we eventually did get to chat, the first thing I asked was, 'What made you create a voicemail message like that?'

Shane told me,

> Myke, there's a lot of ordinary in the world. We so easily get stuck in the day-to-day grind and see everything as generic and boring. But there's no need for that. We can bring the extraordinary and put it in the ordinary.

He went on,

> Every moment is an opportunity to make something special. I really wanted to give people that opportunity. To grab hold of the moment and make something with it.

I asked him what kind of messages he's received. He said,

> Well to start with I'd get the more obvious stuff. The weather, no traffic, health and happiness of friends and family. But then I started getting some really moving messages.

> One guy was grateful for his marriage counsellor as the work they'd done with him and his wife saved their marriage. Another person shared about the inheritance they'd received from a grandparent passing which resulted in them buying their own home, which they thought they'd never be able to do.

> And a friend of mine was so inspired after hearing it, he started a gratitude practice with his kids as

part of their bedtime routine. Every time he tucks them in, he'll ask them what they were grateful for during the day. Then he'll share his and the daily ritual has brought them closer together.

He went on,

Some people even hang up then call back a few hours later once they'd had time to think about it. They really want to leave meaningful answers.

I asked him what this experience was having on him and Shane replied,

After the first few messages I found it such an enriching experience, I started writing them down. Every time I get a new one, I'll pull out the Notes app on my iPhone and capture what someone had said. I'm even thinking about making a book out of them.

This simple intervention packs a powerful punch. Shane is giving people a temporary oasis amidst the frenetic pace of modern life. A quiet, unexpected moment to pause and reflect on what (and who) matters to them. To snap people out of autopilot and make them feel something.

He's also keeping a sense of gratitude ever-present in his own life. Every time he listens to his messages, he's fortunate enough to hear another beautiful story from a friend or colleague, bringing untold joy and delight to his own day-to-day life.

But he's also created an astonishing way to build rapport with strangers and potential clients. Each caller can end up revealing more of who they are by sharing what (and who) they value.

Before he even meets them, Shane has heard a personal, sometimes vulnerable story. When they do finally speak, they've already got a connection. There is an in-built intimacy. They have something meaningful to talk about aside from the generic conversations we default to at work and in life.

And all this from just five words: 'What are you grateful for?'

Harness the feels

This is a critical factor to being an Everyday Creative. To see every moment, every task, every challenge or interaction with another as an opportunity to move them emotionally. To surprise and delight, and snap them out of business as usual. To invite them into a world of beauty, intimacy, serendipity, mystery or gratitude.

Where can you infuse a little more of your personality? Where can you break your unconscious routines, protocols and processes to invite and inspire a little more creativity? Not just in yourself but in the world around you? The benefits extend well beyond your own experience. You might just change the day-to-day experience for someone who really needs it.

So how do we become better at seeing and sensing opportunities to embed more feeling at work? What skills do we need to become an award-winning atmospheric architect and master of vibe design? Where should we look to give ourselves an edge in the esoteric realm of experience?

Aesthetic intelligence

If you are to be effective as an Everyday Creative, and infuse your work with more feeling, meaning and experience, you must become masterful at these three intelligences:

1. **Emotional Intelligence**. The ability to be aware of, control and express your emotions. To handle interpersonal relationships judiciously and empathetically. To know your boundaries and respect the boundaries of others.

2. **Social Intelligence.** The ability to successfully build relationships and navigate social environments. To carry conversations with a wide variety of people, know how to play different roles at different times and be effective in understanding and acting on social cues.

3. **Aesthetic Intelligence.** The ability to understand, interpret and articulate feelings that are elicited by a particular object, environment or experience.

You're probably familiar with the first two but I'd like to focus on the third as I believe it'll give you an unparalleled edge in your work.

Aesthetic intelligence is all about your senses. It's about feeling your way through a situation or circumstance. By accessing your sensory awareness and becoming emotionally attuned to your environment, you develop an ability for deciphering what is meaningful and discerning what matters. You can then use that information when defining and designing your own product, service or experience.

Said another way, it's about tuning in to the vibe, noticing how it makes you feel, deciding which parts light you up, then injecting that magic into whatever you're working on.

Pauline Brown is an adviser to the world's leading luxury brands, a Harvard professor and author of a book appropriately titled *Aesthetic Intelligence*. I met her while speaking at an event in Portugal and I think she's on the cusp of the new wave of business strategy.

In her words,

In a world in which people have cheap and easy access to most goods and services, yet crave richer and more meaningful experiences, aesthetics has become a key differentiator for most companies and a critical factor of their success.

She continues, 'Aesthetic Intelligence provides a crucial roadmap to help business leaders build their business in their own authentic and distinctive way.'

When considering the application of aesthetics in business and life, it's like walking into a new world of possibilities. It gives you a unique way of seeing and perceiving the world so that you can shape a product, environment or interaction to be more beautiful, more meaningful and, ultimately, more influential.

When you apply aesthetic intelligence at work, your emails and spreadsheets, meetings and events, pitch decks and performance reviews all become rich opportunities for engineering a deep, visceral and sensorial experience.

To become more aesthetically intelligent Pauline outlines a four-step process:

1. Begin with **attunement**. You must develop a higher consciousness and deeper awareness of your environment and its affect on you, both emotionally and sensorially. (That is, tune in to how you feel.)

2. Move to **interpretation**. You must translate your emotional reactions (both positive and negative) into ideas that form the basis of an aesthetic position, preference or expression. (That is, express to how you feel.)

3. Then onto **articulation**. Using the sensory data you've received you then define the aesthetic ideals for your brand, product, or service and communicate it to your team so that they not only grasp the vision but can execute on it with precision.

4. And finally, **curation**. You organise, integrate and edit a wide variety of inputs and ideals to achieve maximum impact.

I'll give you an example of when social, emotional and aesthetic intelligences are combined and put in action.

You have a meeting coming up. First, get clear on what you want to achieve from the gathering. Then reflect on what kind of experience you believe would influence that outcome.

Then you consider the people you need to invite. What is the context they exist in? What context will they be in before your meeting? Who are they, what are the factors that shape how they show up and can you influence them in some way?

Then consider the space you're meeting in. Does it align with your intent? Will it elevate and enhance the kind of atmosphere you believe will evoke the kind of conversations you desire? Are you having a blue-sky strategy session in a claustrophobic meeting room with grey walls, a low ceiling and no natural light? Maybe not...

Consider these questions:

≈ How will they feel when they first walk in?

≈ Where will they sit?

≈ Where do you want them to sit?

≈ Do you even want them to sit?

≈ How will you open your meeting?

≈ How will you establish an agreed-upon set of behaviours for the meeting to be effective?

≈ And how do you plan to shape and sculpt the atmosphere as you move through space and time?

Now you're in the meeting. You're fully present to the moment, while remaining subtly detached from it. You're nudging and prodding the energy of the room, while accepting wherever it goes is where it needs to go.

You're holding your intent with soft hands, remaining gently focused on your agenda while responding appropriately to whatever emerges by leveraging your senses and trusting your instincts.

If this sounds like a lot of work, you're right! But it's a different kind of work. It's complex and creative. It requires that you crystallise your intent, empathise with your audience and synthesise the emotional data as it emerges.

You can go even further, and I really hope you do. For example, how do you prepare people for your meetings? How do you invite them?

≈ With a Google calendar link?

≈ With a text?

≈ With a hastily written message on the whiteboard in the lunchroom?

≈ Or with handwritten note you left on their laptops? (Yes!)

≈ Or a digital map that tells them where the treasure (a.k.a. meeting) is, complete with sea monsters and pirates? (Yes, yes!)

≈ Or a line of jelly beans from their desk to the meeting room? (Wow!)

If that all sounds a little too kindergarten for you, I get it. You don't have to go so arts and crafts. But consider how you'd feel if you unexpectedly discovered a glittery gold envelope in your handbag. Inside was a small card that said:

11am. Front Door. SOS

Or how about:

You have been approved for membership.

Meet us at 2.57 pm in the storage room on the 28th floor.

Tell no-one.

Would you be intrigued? Would you feel special? Would you do everything you could to shift your other 3 pm meeting to make that one? I think you would.

An Everyday Creative has a PhD in vibe design. They are atmospheric architects, energetic alchemists and social artisans. They tune in to the world around them, and use their senses and their experiences to create beautiful, visceral and meaningful moments.

Feel like a DJ

DJs, chefs, interior designers—they work with their senses to shift and shape the atmosphere of a rave, restaurant or room. They have a deep desire to move and affect people in a particular way. They take great care in considering:

≈ who their audience is

≈ where they're coming from

≈ what their unmet expectations were or unconscious aspirations are.

That's what you need to do.

I'm not telling you to write up a bunch of psychographic profiles on the people you share an office with. This is about ripping open your heart and letting the raw power of people affect you. It's about tuning in to the hidden secrets of the products, services and experiences that you touch. This is more than mere marketing.

When you start shaping the vibe of your office in emotional, sensory and aesthetic ways, they won't know what hit 'em. They might even start to see you as some kind of witch doctor working with the dark arts. It's powerful. You'll soon discover how influential you can be in any situation or environment.

So how do we begin to unlock the murky, misunderstood realm of feeling? From where should you launch your newfound focus on deciphering and designing meaningful experiences?

Start with how you feel

Let yourself be moved by your experience. Listen with your body and learn to trust your gut. No-one else has to know. It's between you and yourself. But give yourself permission to go there. To play with your senses and fully experience what is emerging in you, in the conversation or in the atmosphere around it.

To be truly effective as an Everyday Creative, you must rebuild the dialogue between your thoughts and your feelings. They need to work in tandem, like shift workers, high-fiving as they go. Imagine the possibilities for your career, if you could draw on the entirety of your human experience, dropping in and out of thinking and feeling whenever it serves.

It's as easy as asking yourself a few simple questions before you make a call, start your next project or design a program:

≈ How does this make me feel?

≈ How do I want this to feel?

≈ How do I want them (clients, colleagues, audience) to feel?

≈ Where else have I felt that?

≈ What was it about that other experience that made me feel that?

≈ What can I take from that experience and infuse into this one?

For example, before sending an email ask yourself:

≈ How do I want them to feel when they receive this?

≈ What would it take for me to make them feel like that?

≈ Where else have I felt like that and can I use it in this context?

After you've written your email, read it through and ask yourself:

≈ How would it make me feel if I received this?

≈ How would it make them (the recipient) feel if they received this?

If it's not aligned, keep going. Sink deeper into your senses and experiment.

You can apply this line of thinking–feeling to every aspect of your job. Every interaction with your customers or colleagues. Every touchpoint of your project or pitch.

> **Making time to consider how you make others feel, how you want them to feel and how to close that gap is crucial to your work as an Everyday Creative.**

A few figures to consider

Just before we get to the activities, here are a couple of interesting facts about feeling that you can use to have more impact at work.

Researchers have discovered that 50 per cent of the most enjoyable elements of an experience are down to anticipation. The other 50 per cent? It's how we remember it.

In a related concept, Daniel Kahneman and Barbara Frederick came up with the Peak/End rule, which refers to the fact that, when reflecting on any experience, our brain will always remember the peak moment and the ending. This is why singing teachers always place great emphasis on how you finish a note or phrase. You can sing the whole song beautifully, but if your finish was sloppy, that's what the audience will remember.

How can you apply this insight to your work? Are you leveraging the power of anticipation? Are you sowing seeds in the days or weeks prior to your meeting or project? Building momentum with a series of carefully curated activations to elicit positive feelings of anticipation and enthusiasm?

Have you determined what your peak moment will be? You can't always know ahead of time, but you can plan for it or stay open to it.

A final consideration

If you're still sitting on the fence about whether you should leap head-first into the wild, wonderful world of feeling, answer me this.

Who would you prefer to work with? Someone who is attuned to your emotional state, who is willing to work with you, and shift their style or approach to meet or match your needs...or someone who just ploughs though, unaware or unconcerned about the impact their behaviour might have on you or what emotional state you might be in due to other forces?

Who would you rather be led by? Someone who shares their vulnerabilities and makes it safe for you to share yours, someone who encourages you to articulate how you feel without judgement or expectation...or someone who tries to keep emotion out of it, prefers to keep things 'professional' and never reveals how they feel about anything?

TIME TO PLAY

Choose one of these to action this week.

1. **Feel first.** Before you begin an email, host a meeting or design a program, ask yourself: How do I want it to feel? Make the experience your primary focus, then build everything around it in a way that fulfils that intention.

2. **Tune in to your senses.** Become more attuned to how the world influences your emotions. Every time you use a product or service, interact with someone, or walk into a new environment, notice how it makes you feel. Try to decipher why it makes you feel that way and take notes. Keep these insights close and use them as a rich databank for shaping your ideas and intentions at work.

3. **Ask them how they feel.** Customers, colleagues, strangers, friends. Your kids, your grandparents, your barista or bus driver. Take your conversation beyond the weather or weekend plans. Ask them open-ended questions about why they like the things they like. Why they chose the outfit they're wearing. What they love (or hate) most about their experience at work. Enquiring and celebrating how they feel legitimises their experience. It gives them permission to tune in to their senses, to trust their instincts, to follow their flavour. You're inviting them to participate in the entire spectrum of their human experience.

4. **Borrow, blend and bastardise.** Feeling isn't just limited to work. Most of your inspiration can and should come from experiences and environments outside the traditional business landscape. The next time you're at a restaurant, tune in to your senses. Bring a mindful awareness to how you feel when you arrive. When you first walk in, who are you greeted by? How are you greeted, and how does it make you feel? Tune in to

the atmosphere in the restaurant: what is the distance between your table and the tables around you? How does that make you feel? Is there music playing? What is it, and does it make you feel energetic and excited? Or relaxed and comfortable? How can you repurpose these experiences in your own work?

5. **Go see some art.** For maximum inspo, spend a little time with those who work exclusively with the senses. Those who are masterful at moving us emotionally, and using Aesthetic Intelligence in its many forms. Go to a gallery, book tickets to the theatre, listen to some live music or borrow a bunch of fiction books from the library. See what you can learn, adopt and repurpose from the masters of feeling.

CHAPTER SIX

The Courage To Make

Develop a bias *for action*

Imagine a house. Nestled into a mountain, high above the cloud line. From where you're standing there's no way for you to see it. You can only imagine it. But the vision fascinates you. Everything you've ever wanted is in that house. You feel it's where you belong.

Before you lies a myriad pathways. Some lead up, some lead down. Some have signs, some are unmarked. There is no way for you to know which one leads directly to the house. So you wait. You wait for others to show you the way. You wait for clear weather. You pack and repack and repack your bag, hoping you'll have everything you might need along the way.

But still you wait.

As the days, weeks and months roll by, the image of the house starts to fade. You don't feel as strongly about making the journey anymore. There are other things that demand your attention, boxes to tick, errands to run, inboxes to empty. You're just so busy now, and besides, it was just a silly dream.

One day, you forget about the house altogether. All the feelings that came with it are no longer with you.

That is, until you unexpectedly meet someone who has just returned from the mountain. Someone who tells you about their house. Someone who looks different, sounds different, feels different.

Something deep in you stirs. A resonant vibration that is as disorienting as it is delicious. The vision comes back. You've been given another chance. Will you take it?

You want to heed the call but there's so many unanswered questions. What if you choose the wrong path, take the wrong turn, get lost along the way? What if you end up further away from where you were originally planning to go? What if you never make it or never make it back?

You turn to the stranger, grab them by the arm and say, 'You gotta tell me which path should I take?' They smile, put their hand on your shoulder and whisper, 'My friend, I can't help you with that. All I can tell you is to just start walking...'

'... the way will reveal the way.'

I'm sure you have dreams of your own metaphorical house. Audacious aspirations of a faraway destination. A bold creative project, a daring career move. A deep impulse to make something that asks you to trade the safety of what you know for the danger of what you don't.

But so often you get stopped before you even get started. Overwhelmed by the options. Paralysed by the possibilities. Instead of getting stuck into the difficult work ahead, you settle for what's convenient, grow attached to what's comfortable, accept that what you have is good enough for now.

What we misunderstand most about making is that the map we think we need is only ever revealed by making it. The clarity we seek never arrives; it is *created*. And that the only way to know if a hunch is worth taking, or a dream is worth making, is to make it.

What it means to make

In the context of an Everyday Creative, 'making' is not limited to physical objects or artefacts. Not restricted to performances or commercial projects. You can make a moment. Make a relationship. Make a career. But to do so requires a shift in your being.

A maker has a bias for action. An addiction to participation. An obsession with the process of creation.

Their vision for a particular outcome might propel them to pick up their tools. But it's their love of playing and rearranging, mixing and switching, combining and realigning raw materials that keeps them going.

Making, by its very nature, is about movement. It's dynamic and responsive, flexible and adaptive, fluid and open to change. To make is to be resourceful and regenerative. To use whatever is available to you to build something new. In essence, it's the natural expression of our unique human potential and breathes new energy into our work and life.

So why do we find it so bloody hard?

F.E.A.R.

Yes, fear. Did you really think we'd get through an entire book on creativity without talking about fear?

Neuroscientists call it the amygdala, Seth Godin calls it The Lizard Brain, Steven Pressfield calls it The Resistance. You might simply call it writer's block. Whatever you call it personally, its effects are the same.

It stops us.

From taking the first step, from putting pen to paper, from making the call or booking the venue. Though its intent is noble (to keep us safe), ironically, fear has blood on its hands. Killing our dreams, suffocating our desires, murdering the promise of our muse.

So much has already been written about fear. Susan Jeffers ordered us to 'feel the fear and do it anyway'. Suzy Kassem reminded us that 'doubt kills more dreams than failure ever will', and Franklin D. Roosevelt told us 'the only thing to fear is fear itself'.

Until we develop neurological implants to numb its effects, fear is just a part of being human. A biological response to any real or perceived threats. And nothing is more threatening than making. Why?

Ideas are powerful. They have the potential to change minds, topple governments, disrupt entire industries. But an idea is still just an idea. Without action, nothing happens.

But when we *make*, we are changing the nature of reality. Making the abstract concrete. Confining all potentialities to a one-way street. The process of making is to hold infinity in one hand and specificity in the other. Of course this feels unsettling.

As the Danish philosopher Søren Kierkegaard wrote in 1844, 'the inevitable result of passing over from a state of possibility into one of actuality is a sense of anxiety'. In this intermediate state, fear is both natural and necessary. But for reasons that go well beyond a generic platitude on an Instagram meme.

When we make, we're signing our name to something tangible that can be weighed and measured. We're not just declaring an intent; we're delivering an outcome. We're creating something real that leaves us open to the judgement of others.

And that's terrifying.

What if what we make turns out to be not so great? What if what we do closes more doors than it opens? What if we get stuck with something we don't want or the world doesn't like? What will they say about us?

Beyond our fear of judgement, of being deemed unworthy or unlovable, what we really fear is being responsible. Accountable to what we've made and what our making will make of us.

Take procreation. The idea of having kids is one thing. The reality is another thing entirely. When that sperm hits that egg it sets off a chain of events that you cannot anticipate. And once that baby's born there's no going back, no undo button, no control-alt-delete.[34]

You're accountable for your actions and responsible for the outcomes that are a result of them.

Think about it like this. Before you make anything, your mind is weighing up this equation:

≈ If I choose to make this idea, I will almost certainly change the reality I currently exist in.

≈ I can't predict the precise outcome of my creative process but the odds are it won't be anything like I had originally intended.

≈ And no matter happens, I am responsible for whatever I bring into this world. I must sign my name on the bottom of the page and own the effects and impact of what I made.

Heavy. It makes sense that we'd hesitate, research, analyse and procrastinate. It's perfectly normal to think that the best course of action would be to make a *plan* of action before we *take* any action.

If we're going to play with that scenario, we need a guarantee. Especially when the stakes are high or when money is tight (i.e. pretty much every day in the office). If we have to own the outcome we've got to give ourselves the best shot at success by mitigating as much of the risk as possible.

Or do we…

---

[34] This is the moment you lose control of the TV remote, you start leaving parties at 2 pm (not 2 am) and never get to enjoy going to the bathroom alone ever again.

The risks of mitigating risk

A pre-determined plan, a considered approach, a thoroughly researched strategy ... Surely they're all assets when it comes to taking calculated risks? Any rational, reasonable person can see that it's foolish to move forward on any project without a clear idea of where you're going!

Maybe. But it can also be a danger when we try too hard to make it safe to make.

Miss the moment

Life moves fast. Business moves even faster. There are windows of opportunity. Seasons of suitability. Fleeting moments when the conditions for an idea are 'just right'. If you don't act the chances are the market will move. The budget gets cut. A colleague takes leave. With every change in circumstances the original possibility becomes harder until it's nearly impossible to make.

Cast your mind back to a time when you were part of a great team or had a brilliant boss, or could see an exciting opportunity before anyone else. Did you throw yourself into the moment? Did you get started before you knew how to finish? Did you jump in the deep end without knowing the depth?

Or did you hesitate, choosing to gather more information? To wait for buy-in, or approval, or for the conditions to be a little more favourable?

What happened when you dived in? What happened when you didn't?

Dilute the dream

Another risk of mitigating risk is that you end up diluting the dream. You rework the numbers. Rehash the desired outcome. Reposition the anticipated results until you end up with something far more reasonable and far more achievable. By lowering the bar, you tell yourself there's a higher probability of success.

The problem is, your bold, beautiful vision starts to look awfully like what you've already got. With all the slashing and rehashing your idea starts to feel painfully familiar.

Over time it gets harder to stay inspired by its potential. You become less motivated to see it through, and ultimately underwhelmed by the final result. You end up with a project so tame and so lame that even if it is delivered as it was designed (and it never is), it doesn't make any significant difference. You end up with work you're neither proud of nor inspired by.

Just another day at the office.

Embody the enemy

But the real threat of trying to smooth out all the bumps, prepare for every pitfall and alleviate all the risk is that you wind up embracing the things you used to resist. You get comfortable being comfortable. You settle for the safety of the status quo.

Pretty soon, you're the one asking to see the ROI. *You're* the one who 'just isn't sure if it's a good time right now'. *You're* the one who suggests to the team, 'we should probably test that idea first. In a smaller market. With no real budget or support.'[35]

Consider this. No one was born boring. No one had dreams of being a buzz-kill. It happens slowly, subtly and insidiously. Little compromises, tiny retreats, seemingly innocuous excuses. If you don't find the courage to make, chances are you'll wake up one day behind enemy lines. Dressed just like your adversary and sounding exactly the same as the detractors you used to rally against.

---

[35] Now don't get me wrong. Starting small is a great thing. And so is doing your due diligence. But it's a fine line. We're working against the oldest part of our brain and it's very, *very* good at selling its story.

The antidote

Here's the reality. You will not know if your ideas are any good until you bring them to life. You will never know what you're truly capable of until you jump in the ring. You will not enjoy the life and career you desire and deserve until you make it.

I'm going to give you a collection of ways to start, continue *and* finish what you want to make. But all of them are underpinned by one core idea: action. Finding the courage to make is about developing a bias for action.

You have to get in the habit of raising your hand *before* you have a question. You've got to sign your name at the bottom of an empty page, and then fill it, with reckless, relentless abandon. You might feel like an imposter, unqualified or unprepared, but that's exactly as you should feel.

In the words of the great David Bowie,

If you feel safe in the area that you're working in, you're not working in the right area. Always go a little further into the water than you feel you're capable ... [when] your feet aren't quite touching the bottom you're just about in the right place to do something exciting.

On Starting

Fill the space, fast!

The simplest strategy to *start* making is … wait for it …

To make something. (#facepalm)

Seriously. Just do something.[36] Anything. A splash of paint on the canvas. A single word on the page. Move one solitary chair onto the stage. But do it quickly. It's vital to make the length of time between when you get an idea and when you feel compelled to make as short as possible.

Why?

≈   Fear loves time. The more it has, the better it gets at refining its message.

≈   Blank space is debilitating. When starting, too much possibility can be lethal.

In 2006, Barry Schwartz published a book called *The Paradox of Choice*. He built his ideas on surprising research that emerged in 2000, and brought concept of *analysis paralysis* into the mainstream.

When you have all these choices, you have an enormous problem gathering all the information to decide which is the right one. You start looking over your shoulder, thinking that if you'd made a different choice, you'd have done better. So there's regret, which makes you less satisfied with what you have chosen, whether or not there's good reason to have regrets. It's easy to imagine there was a better option, even if there wasn't really, because you can't possibly examine all of them.

The paradox of choice lurks behind every blank page. And every extra minute spent reflecting on possibilities weakens your impulse to make. So just start. By doing anything, fast.

---

[36] This was actually the title of my first book—*Just do Something: A Guidebook for Turning Dreamers into Makers*

Book a gig. Pay in full.

Building on this idea, another effective way to start making is to engineer a scenario that you can't back out of. If you want to host an event, pick a date, book a venue and pay the invoice in full. You want to leverage a potential loss in cash or reputation by putting skin in the game.

When I think back on all the bands I've been in, the ones that started because of a gig (that is, I'd already booked a show before I had organised a band) were way more successful than those that started with a vague idea or starry-eyed intention.

Knowing I had very little time to find musicians, rehearse a few songs and perform on a specific date was a powerful motivator. Again, cash, reputation and pride were on the line.

The bands that started as an idea rarely got off the ground. We'd spend months in rehearsals, writing and rewriting songs, getting hung up on band names or bios. Without the urgency of a gig or the thrill of a live performance, we'd inevitably lose interest. All that potential, all that work, wasted.

This is another way of saying, deadlines are lifelines.

Don't be afraid to overcommit, to agree to something that makes no sense, to architect a set of circumstances that force you to show up whether you're ready or not. Because at the very least, you will have started.

THE UNWRITTEN ROAD

I feel a bit naughty saying this. I don't want to play favourites, but if I had to ... Aimee Coleman would have to be my #1 most favourite client ever.

When we met, Aimee was frustrated at work, terrified of living a 'paint-by-numbers' life and searching for the missing link that would set her soul on fire.

For Aimee, that meant creative writing. She was an author, novelist and poet — she just didn't have a whole lot of proof of that yet.

(continued)

THE UNWRITTEN ROAD (cont'd)

Our plan was to get her writing (anything and fast), especially as she'd already quit her job and in three months would be backpacking around the world for an indeterminate period of time.

In one of our sessions I remember Aimee saying, 'Ahhh, I'm just not sure Myke? Perhaps we should put this program on hold. It might be a bit hard for me to write when I'm away. Maybe we can start this process again when I return.'

'Nope!' I replied. 'That would be a perfectly legitimate excuse and Everyday Creatives like us have an aversion to those.'

It was at that point, over our second pint, we hatched a plan to get Aimee writing. Not a few lines a day or a few hours a week. We decided she would write her first novel while she traversed the globe.

Every week, she'd write a chapter and email it to her growing database (which at that time comprised of her family, a few friends and me). Then when (or if) she returned to Melbourne, she'd publish and launch her novel at an event.

In Aimee's mind, she had no right to be a novelist. She didn't have a degree in creative writing, nor had she 'paid her dues' by publishing short stories on a blog for years. So the thought of doing this was delightfully dangerous.

But life is short, creativity is the shiz and with a little nudge Aimee decided to go after the exact thing she wanted most. A novel.

And you know the best part of this story? She bloody did it!

That crazy, wild, spirited soul found the courage to write and share her work every single day. Despite the millions of justifiable reasons that could've stopped her, she wrote, she published and launched her book *Something From Nothing*, and I have never been so proud of anyone in my life.

When I spoke to Aimee about sharing her story in this book she told me,

I always wanted to be a writer, but I was waiting for permission. I came to you hoping you'd give me the formula. A fool-proof, step by step process to becoming one.

But I realised I can't follow your story. I can't do what I want to do by doing what you did. We've had very different lives, come from different cultures and backgrounds. We have different stories to tell. And it's these differences that give you your own voice. You have to do it on your own. There was never going to be a step by step process to follow.'

When I asked her how she'd changed as a result of the project, she told me,

If you'd asked me if I was self-conscious before writing the book I'd have said no, but looking back, I was. I was really reluctant to share anything online, or have an opinion about something. But now, I love it. I love having an opinion, sharing ideas, and putting myself out there. That side of the process is now a big part of the joy I find in creating.

And now I recognise that if a story comes to me, it deserves to be told. Who am I to stop it from being out there in the world? I learned first hand that if you put your intention out there, and begin to take action toward it, the universe will arrange itself around you.

Once Aimee returned, published and launched her book,[37] she was contacted by her old boss. He wanted her to come back, offered her a place on the management team and with

(continued)

---

[37] You can see more of Aimee's story, watch a deep interview I did with her and see a video I made of her book launch by checking out the resources section of the website—www.everydaycreatives.com.

THE UNWRITTEN ROAD (cont'd)

her newfound confidence she easily negotiated a four-day week to allow time for her writing.

I asked her how this process had affected her other work and she said,

> Well I've noticed I'm softer with people now. I'm not looking for perfection in the people I work with and lead. I understand what it takes to put your self and your ideas out there so I can empathise with others wherever they are on their journey.

> But I had this romantic idea of what a writer is or does. And I really thought my life needed to look like that. I realised I can be more than one thing. I can have more than one career. Express myself in a multitude of ways. I actually really enjoy thinking logically. I find solving real-world problems very satisfying and being around other people is really important to me.

> So when my old boss heard I was back, and he asked if I would rejoin the company, I was actually quite excited about it. Especially as he offered me a spot on the management team and I negotiated a four-day week to allow time for my writing!

So Aimee quit her job to travel the world. Wrote a novel while on the road, then published and launched it on her return. Once her old boss heard about all this, he begged her to come back by offering her more money and more responsibility while working less time.

No matter what happens from here, Aimee is an author. She wrote, published and launched her novel. And no-one can ever take that away from her.

When you make, the whole world changes.

And what is she up to now? She's already halfway through her next book.

On Continuing

Keep it close

Once you're up and running, the battle is far from over. Maintaining your momentum is essential if you're going to keep yourself making.

James Clear, author of the international bestseller *Atomic Habits*, writes, 'motivation is overrated; environment matters more'. What he means is, when we're trying to build a new habit (like becoming a maker), we need to redesign our environment to trigger our desired behaviour. We need to make it easy.

For example, if you want to exercise more, putting your gym clothes next to the bed at night is a good idea. Sleeping in your running shoes is even better. If you want to keep making, you need to keep it close. Visible and within arm's reach as much as possible.

I'm a piano player by trade, but I've always had a desire to play classical guitar. In the past, I'd wait for times when no-one was at home to practise. I'd pull my acoustic out of its case and get an hour or so to myself to work on my technique.

Because those moments were so few and far between, I'd spend the first half an hour frustrated, trying to regain where I left off a week, month or year ago. It wasn't until I decided to keep it out of its case that I started making progress.

Leaving my guitar in the living room, lying on the couch, always within eyesight and arm's reach meant that my goal of developing my guitar skills was always present. I found myself playing every day. I picked it up when I walked past, when I sat down, when I was waiting for the kettle to boil. As a result, I improved my technical ability, increased my enjoyment of playing and even boosted my personal pride by knowing I was working toward my goal.

Whatever project you're working on (even if that project is you and your own creative recovery), keep it close. Keep it out of its case and always somewhere within reach. You want to see it, feel it and touch it every single day.

There are no wrong notes

There aren't a whole lot of straight lines on the path to everyday creativity. Inevitably, as you start to make you'll encounter an endless array of mishaps. Even the best of us can be derailed by a mix-up or a mistake. So what should you do when you find yourself face to face with a failure or a full-tilt f@#k up?

Herbie Hancock is one of the greatest musicians of all time. He's spent the better part of 60 years mastering and innovating music. He tells a story about playing with the great Miles Davis that I try to work into every keynote I deliver. I think it's one of the greatest approaches to creativity and life I've ever heard. It captures the essence of jazz and offers a powerful mindset to embrace when in the madness of making. As Herbie said,

> **... we were playing 'So what' ... and I played the wrong chord. It sounded like a big mistake ... Miles paused for a second then played some notes that made my chord right ... Since he didn't hear it as a mistake, he felt it was his responsibility to find something that fit.**

To not hear, see or feel mistakes as mistakes takes profound discipline. Not the discipline we naturally think of when we hear that word. It's not ruling with an iron fist, it requires no furrowed brow. It's the discipline to accept what is. To soften, open and embrace. Whatever emerges isn't just okay. It's exactly what was supposed to be.

Where Miles really shows us the value and power of making is when he 'felt it was his responsibility to find something that fit'. He didn't get mad at Herbie.

He didn't write a passive aggressive email, bitch about him later that night to his wife and avoid him for three weeks. He took responsibility for it. He paused, shifted his approach and made Herbie's chord sound right. He turned a mistake into a melody. Be like Miles, and infuse any faults or failures into the final product.

On Finishing

Done is better than perfect

The only thing more important than starting and continuing is *finishing*. Without finishing there's a high probability you'll get stuck in the mud of your making. Relentlessly revising your work until it's unrecognisable from the original. Second-guessing your choices and justifying another delayed deadline. This is precisely where the peril of perfectionism rears its ironically ugly head.

An Everyday Creative knows that it's vital to commit to the close. To find the courage to put down the tools, call last drinks and hit send.

The author Anne Lamott said it well in her book on writing, *Bird by Bird*,

Perfectionism is the voice of the oppressor, the enemy of the people. It will keep you cramped and insane your whole life. I think perfectionism is based on the obsessive belief that if you run carefully enough, hitting each stepping-stone just right, you won't have to die. The truth is that you will die anyway and that a lot of people who aren't even looking at their feet are going to do a whole lot better than you, and have a lot more fun while they're doing it.

Man, I love that. Especially the part about people who appear to care less about what they're creating (compared to us) yet they seem to have 20 times more fun. Their indifference to 'getting it right' liberates them from the clutches of perfection and enables them to just get on with it. To make something else. To be reckless and relentless with their work.

While reflecting on how I get to *done* and researching how others get to *done*, I came across a blog post appropriately titled 'The Cult of Done Manifesto'.

It was written back in 2009 by two authors (Bre Pettis and Kio Stark) who had recently started dating. They were lying in bed one morning, talking about the negative effects of perfectionism and sharing strategies they both used to overcome it, when they decided to put their thoughts to paper. To write and share a manifesto that *anyone* could use to help get their work *done*.

The best part: they gave themselves just 20 minutes to write it before they posted it online.[38]

What I love most about their manifesto is that it's not perfect. Some of the sentences are a little ambiguous. Some don't quite make sense. But it's done. They wrote it in 20 minutes, posted it online and here we are talking about it over a decade later.

Enjoy.

THE CULT OF DONE MANIFESTO

≈ There are three states of being. Not knowing, action and completion.

≈ Accept that everything is a draft. It helps to get it done.

≈ There is no editing stage.

≈ Pretending you know what you're doing is almost the same as knowing what you are doing, so just accept that you know what you're doing even if you don't and do it.

≈ Banish procrastination. If you wait more than a week to get an idea done, abandon it.

≈ The point of being done is not to finish but to get other things done.

≈ Once you're done you can throw it away.

≈ Laugh at perfection. It's boring and keeps you from being done.

(continued)

---

[38] I highly recommend checking out the original post, 'The Cult of Done Manifesto' on Medium.com.

THE CULT OF DONE
MANIFESTO (cont'd)

≈ People without dirty hands are wrong. Doing something makes you right.

≈ Failure counts as done. So do mistakes.

≈ Destruction is a variant of done.

≈ If you have an idea and publish it on the internet, that counts as a ghost of done.

≈ Done is the engine of more.

Begin again, again

Best-selling novelist and creativity advocate Neil Gaiman says, 'You have to finish things—that's what you learn from, you learn by finishing things.' What he means is, until you stop, get a little distance between you and your work, you're still in it. You can't view it objectively. You're still thinking about how to improve that particular thing as opposed to reflecting on what you can take from that experience and apply to your next project.

The key here is to have another project that demands your attention. You need to have something else that you need to start working on and, until you finish this one, you can't start that one.

Personally, I like to tell myself my fifth book will be the bestseller. And the only way to get to the fifth, is to write and finish the second, third and fourth. I can't tell you how many times I applied this mindset to writing the book you're reading right now. Honestly, the only way I managed to finish this thing was by telling myself that the next one will be better. And the one after that will be better still.

How can you apply this approach to your work?

What is the project you'd love to do later? The big, bold, brilliant one. The one that requires a bunch of skills, talents and experience you don't quite possess just yet. Skills and experience you'll probably attain through the project you're working on right now. Well, hurry up and finish this one, so you can get to the next one. And the one after that, and the one after that!

A final thought

To make is gutsy. You move from the grandstand into the game, from side of stage into the spotlight. From dreaming and scheming to actively re-creating the world around you. Of all the four practices, making is by far the most difficult.

And here's the brutal, beautiful truth. You were never invited to play. You don't belong on that stage. And you are nowhere near ready. You never will be. No-one is. The magic of making is reserved for those who are brave enough to say yes, to take the mic and start to sing.

Everyday Creatives don't often seek permission and rarely wait for approval. They don't have precise plans, nor do they execute them perfectly. Their only focus is on playing the first note. And the note after that. For them the process is the outcome, the joy is in the journey.

You will never know if your ideas are any good until you bring them to life. You will never know what you're truly capable of until you put some skin in the game. You will never enjoy the career and life you desire and deserve until you start making it.

TIME TO PLAY

Choose one of these to action this week ...

1. Just make something.

CHAPTER SEVEN

The Courage
To Give

Embodying a *spirit of generosity*

Darren Hill is a behavioural scientist, executive director and award-winning educator with broad shoulders, bold ambitions and a big heart. In 2019, he wanted to take his professional creativity to the next level. His vision was to write and perform a keynote for a national roadshow of events. It involved two spoken-word pieces, a daring video sync[39] and an unconventional guided meditation on death.

I loved the weekly call with Daz, getting an update on where he was on his creative journey. More than a few times he talked about pulling the pin. 'Maybe it's just not ready', he said. 'I'm not sure if I'll do it justice. I just haven't had enough time to prepare.'

I'm sure you can relate.

From the dizzying heights of possibility to the harrowing despair of inadequacy; the promise of adoration to the threat of humiliation. He was riding that creative rollercoaster, at full speed without a seatbelt, and it was glorious.

---

[39] He wanted to integrate and interact with pre-recorded video vignettes woven throughout his performance.

D-day came and after his first sizzling performance, a delegate approached him in the break. He shared with Darren that he'd planned on ending his life that morning. That he'd run out of reasons to keep living but somehow dragged himself to the conference. After seeing Darren's presentation, he found a new hope, a new possibility for his life and a meaningful reason to keep living.

If Darren had quit when his creative process got tough—if he'd have waited until he felt ready, compromised his creative vision or reverted to a regular old keynote—would he have had the same impact? We'll never know.

What we do know is that he saved a life that day. And all the work he'd done, all the pressure and anxiety he felt, all the courage it took to step through the fear and give his work to the world was worth it.

You will never know the impact you can have by giving your creativity to the world.

As an Everyday Creative, it's not your job to judge the value of what you create. It's not up to you to decide if what you've made is worthy or ready. Your job is just to make things, then give them away. To set your ideas, projects and art free. To be generous with your approach, abundant with your attitude and relentless in your commitment to contribute.

A spirit of generosity

If you asked a large group of people to outline the essential elements of creativity, you'd be hard pressed to find a list that didn't include:

≈ curiosity

≈ courage

≈ open-mindedness

≈ independence

≈ innovation

≈ playfulness

≈ positivity

≈ energy.

You might even find focus, motivation and discipline somewhere in the mix.

But generous?

I'm sure you agree that generosity is both important and valuable in life and work—but a key driver of creativity? Consider this: without generosity there is no creativity. If no-one ever shared their ideas, offered up their skills or networks, or gave away the things they made, we wouldn't have much of a world. And we wouldn't have much to work with.

When it comes to creativity, we're all 'standing on the shoulders of giants'. We're building on the ideas and innovations of our colleagues or competitors. We're leveraging the generosity of others, whether we realise it or not. Whether *they* realise it or not.

For an Everyday Creative, generosity isn't just an afterthought, a byproduct or a nice-to-have. It's:

≈ fundamental to how they show up at work

≈ essential for building the relationships that extend and amplify their ideas

≈ vital as a principle and practice in every facet of their career and life.

But … as obvious and admirable as that all sounds, it's not always easy to be so generous. Especially at work, where power dynamics and value exchanges form the fabric of business itself. The way our workplaces are designed, we're all competing for resources, recognition or reward. And given that kind of environment, it's only natural to want to protect our little patch!

However, hoarding our ideas, withholding information or concealing our creative intent isn't just inconsiderate—it's ineffective. Without a spirit of generosity and an attitude of abundance our creative aspirations are dead in the water. If we have a desire to be more creative at work (and we do), we better find a way to get good at giving. *Fast*!

Fortunately, a lot of our resistance to generosity is just the result of a few misguided beliefs. So let's call them out, then look at a couple of simple strategies to ensure generosity is central to the way you operate at work.

Belief #1: We worry that our ideas will be corrupted by others (eek!)

You know the feeling: you're so in love with your vision. So assured of its value. Why risk its potential being squashed or sabotaged by someone else? If you let them join the party there's a high chance they'll just take over or take all the credit.

And some of the time that turns out to be true. But what we misunderstand about giving our ideas away is that there's a strong probability these same people might make our ideas better.

Perhaps they see something we've overlooked or something we underestimated. Their objectivity is an asset. Their presence might bring a new perspective, a new set of tools, or expose you to a wider network.

Those in the online gaming industry are masters at giving to get. They'll often release a game before it's finished with an invitation to their community to find all the bugs, point out all the problems and even rewrite the code to improve their overall experience. Essentially, they're giving their product away before it's perfect, then letting their consumers finish it for them.

Brilliant.

So what else keeps us from sharing our stuff with our team?

Belief #2: We worry that we'll be exploited by others (ouch!)

We've all been heavily conditioned to see work as a series of transactions. Mutual exchanges that require an equal balance of value. If I'm going to give you something, I've got to be sure I get something in return.

Otherwise, I'll be taken advantage of, used and abused, seen as merely a resource to leverage and leave behind.

Research by The Greater Good Science Center for the Templeton Foundation, however, tells us that giving endears us more to the people around us. This results in more positive outcomes for ourselves, both immediately and in the long term.

If you share information readily, credit others consistently and give your time and resources liberally, what comes across to your colleagues is a strong work ethic, great communication skills and a willingness to collaborate.

This inevitably amplifies trust, builds respect and extends a bank of goodwill. Karma that you can return to and draw on in ways you couldn't have if you hadn't already been so generous.

Most of the time though, we don't give our work away for reasons that are far more insidious.

Belief #3: We worry that our ideas are worthless to others (sigh!)

Generally speaking, most of us grossly undervalue our observations and expressions. We misinterpret the merit of our expertise and experience. We decide our work, talent or vision is okay for us but second rate for anyone else.

Have you ever thought up a radical new approach but instead of giving it to the team you kept it to yourself? Only to find out later that your idea would've made the project more successful and enjoyable for both you and the team?

Or have you ever walked off stage after a presentation ready to curl up into a ball, pull the covers over your head and hide for eternity (I have more than once), only to receive overwhelming praise from the audience, leaving you chuffed yet baffled? 'Were they even in the room?' you ask yourself as another enthusiastic fan tells you how fabulous you were.

If there's one thing I've learned over two decades of professional creativity, it's that I'm a terrible judge of my work. And I bet my right arm that you're a terrible judge of yours.

So how do we shift our mindset from scarcity to abundance? How do we transcend the transactional approach we've been conditioned to take? And how do we see our work as worthy and give it away consistently without concern?

Well, first, it's important we separate ourselves from what we create.

It's not us, it's you and me

Elizabeth Gilbert (author of *Eat, Pray, Love* and *Big Magic*) told us during her 2015 TED talk that we should consider detaching ourselves from our work. That by distancing our ideas from our identity, and our expression from our ego, we will liberate ourselves from the pressure of our process and the impact of our output.

By seeing ourselves and our work as two distinct entities that come into contact for a brief time, we're free to work with our muse like a partner or a collaborator. If I am not my project, it's okay if you take it, mess with it and make it your own. You're not doing it to me; you're doing it to the project.

I love this concept and use it frequently. I like to imagine hundreds of ideas flying through the ether at any one time. If I'm lucky, one might choose to come to me. My job is not to judge its value or relevance. Nor is it to believe that it was specifically meant for me and me alone. My job is to decide whether this idea is right for me right now, and, if so, then bring my full creative self to it. To build it in the best way I can, then send it on its way. To work generously with the unrealised intentions of the universe.

This mindset does two things:

1. You won't get sucked into the success or failure of an idea. Which means you won't spend weeks in a hole if what you've created has little to no impact on anyone else. And equally, it will keep you grounded when things go well and for a time you're belle of the ball. It'll help you transcend the hype and steer clear of any hubris.

2. It keeps the channel open. It's easy to get stuck on an idea, trying to perfect it or get it just right. You can lose days, weeks, sometimes even years hanging on too tight to one particular project. But viewing it as separate from yourself allows you to get it out there in the world, decluttering the bench space of your mind. This leaves you open to receiving other strokes of insight that may be the seeds of your next great idea. Be a river, not a dam.

Separating ourselves from our work is an effective strategy for sharing our ideas. But what about coming up with them? Can generosity help us become more innovative and prolific?

Brian Eno, the musician and producer, certainly thinks so. He argues that breakthrough creativity only ever happens inside a specific kind of environment. And that if we focus on cultivating this kind of environment, creativity will be a naturally occurring phenomenon.

He calls this kind of environment a *scenius*.

Scenius

Scenius, according to Eno, is the collective intelligence and intuition that arises organically from a vibrant creative and cultural scene. It's the result of a network of diverse individuals who embody shared principles that drive one another to breakthrough creativity (both individually and collectively).

He uses examples like The Inklings, the Bloomsbury Group, Building 20 at MIT, Silicon Valley (early days), Madchester and Burning Man[40] to make his point, but I'm sure you can think of others: moments in time where a group of individuals came together to make each other better. Perhaps you have had a time in your life when you were unknowingly part of a scenius.

Think back on your career. Was there a particular team, company or a group of friendly competitors that stands out to you? Was there a window of time when creativity flowed freely, when people were comfortable to take more risks, accelerating the success of both the individuals and the group?

Eno insists that this kind of radical innovation is never the result of individual talent but the product of a culture. He posits that...

Genius comes from the scene, rather than the gene.

---

[40] The Inklings were an informal literary circle in Oxford in the 1930s and 1940s. Notable members included C.S. Lewis and J.R.R. Tolkien. The Bloomsbury group was a group of English writers, intellectuals, philosophers and artists including Virginia Woolf, John Maynard Keynes, E.M. Forster and Lyttin Strachy. Building 20 at MIT was originally built as a temporary space to hold scientists during WWII. It was never demolished because there were so many students on campus and it became the epicentre of innovation for brilliant minds like Amar Bose (who founded the Bose Corporation) and linguist Noam Chomsky. Madchester was a rave music and cultural scene that developed in north-west England in the late 1980s. Many famous groups were a product of this time, including the Stone Roses and Happy Mondays. Burning Man is an annual event held in the Black Rock Desert in north-west Nevada. Every year, thousands of people build a temporary city, populated with gigantic art installations and immersive activities.

A scenius is nurtured by four core elements. While reading them, I invite you to reflect on the culture of your current workplace. Does this describe the atmosphere of your team, organisation or industry? Or is there plenty of opportunity for you to inject a few of these characteristics into your workplace culture?

1. **Mutual appreciation.** Risky moves are applauded by the group, subtlety is appreciated, and friendly competition goads the shy. Scenius can be thought of as the best of peer pressure.

2. **Rapid exchange of tools and techniques.** As soon as something is invented, it is flaunted and then shared. Ideas flow quickly because they are flowing inside a common language and sensibility.

3. **Network effects of success.** When a record is broken, a hit happens or breakthrough erupts, the success is claimed by the entire scene. This empowers the scene to further success.

4. **Local tolerance for the novelties.** The local 'outside' does not push back too hard against the transgressions of the scene. The renegades and mavericks are protected by this buffer zone.

What I love most about the concept of a scenius is that it democratises creativity. It makes creativity more accessible and inclusive to all. The more you win, the more I win. The more daring I get, the more daring you get. As soon as you learn something new, it's quickly something I can use.

And, of course, tying it all together is a spirit of generosity.

Isn't this exactly what we want our workplaces to be? Petri dishes of unbridled creativity that build upon the rapid adoption of new skills and ideas?

Austin Kleon, the best-selling author of *Steal Like an Artist*, adds,

Being a valuable part of a scenius is not necessarily about how smart or talented you are, but about what you have to contribute — the ideas you share, the quality of the connections you make, and the conversations you start.

Beautiful. You don't have to be stereotypically 'creative'[41] to be an Everyday Creative, you just have to be willing to contribute. To shift your focus beyond your own success to the success of the collective. To consistently offer up ideas or information, share connections or credit, to give your time, attention and support to the people around you.

It's time to stop worrying about what you can get, and start working on what you can give.

Who would you rather work with, someone who hoards their ideas, withholds important information and conceals their creative aspirations? Or someone who gives away their ideas away, liberally and consistently? Who is always on the lookout for new opportunities to add value to what you're doing? Who never hesitates to split their lunch money, show you a shortcut or let you take the wheel for a while?

No brainer.

Building on this concept of a scenius, and the characteristics of the people who make it possible, there is another place we can look for

---

[41] Complete with a hipster beard, skinny jeans and an overpriced designer laptop case.

inspiration when it comes to giving. The wild, wacky and wonderful world of improv.

Give like an improviser

The principles of improvisation (both in theatre and jazz) have long been regarded as a useful approach in business. You might've even attended a masterclass or experienced an improv activity as part of a conference ice-breaker or warm-up.

People often struggle to understand how it works. They gasp at the immediacy of a song or a scene forming before them, with no script and no rehearsal. But to the improviser, it's simple. You just give. You offer up an idea, you share a melody. And then another. And another. You build with what is offered by others, and they build with what is offered by you.

By design, improvisation embodies all aspects of a scenius in real time. It's generative and inclusive. Generous and dangerous. It's everything we work to cultivate as an Everyday Creative.

Let's take a closer look at a few of the tenets of improv. Again, while you read, reflect on how you might use these elements in your team dynamics.[42] Some tenets of improv are:

≈ **Be present.** Choose to show up fully in each and every moment. Bring your focus and attention to who you're with and what is happening right in front of you. This heightened state of awareness gives you an increased ability to react and adapt, while reassuring your colleagues you're in the moment together.

≈ **Yes, and.** Choose to fully accept any and every reality that emerges, and greet it with a positive and generative response.

---

[42] I'm just giving a high-level overview of improv. I could write a whole book on it and, in fact, many have. If you have a desire to go deeper into the glorious world of improv, I recommend reading *Impro* by Keith Johnstone. For the more musically minded, I recommend *Effortless Mastery* by Kenny Werner. But really, you need to try it out. You can't read your way to improvisational mastery. Find yourself an improv class, go listen to jazz and always volunteer when there is an opportunity to try something that's never been done before.

Interact with what is being offered to you by offering something that is inclusive and participatory by nature.

≈ **Make everyone else look good.** Shift your focus from yourself to everyone else. Lose the burden of competition or defensiveness. Liberate yourself from justifying your decisions and do all you can to help the people around you win (and look fabulous while they do).

≈ **Momentum matters.** Whatever happens, whatever emerges, embrace it and keep the energy going. In life we often stop to analyse or criticise things as they arise. In improv, you trust the process and just keep moving. The entire system is not static—it is alive and dynamic.

≈ **Always serve the song.** Stay anchored to fulfilling the overall process. Remain centred on delivering the overarching project. When you constantly ask yourself, 'How can I best serve this situation?', you won't stray from the original intent of the project, while transcending any temporary impulses for recognition or reward (which stops the flow of energy/creativity).

There's a lot to digest and draw out of those tenets, and that's not even all of them. But the essence of applying this approach in a workplace context is summed up perfectly in an interview in *The New York Times* with Susan Credle, then chief creative officer of Leo Burnett USA. When she was bringing a new team together she said to them at an all-in meeting,

> **You are not competing with each other in here ... I would suggest that if you look at something and you have a better idea, that you generously give that idea to someone and make them better. Because if we all do that, we all win.**

What we're trying to do here is move from …

- ≈ scarcity to abundance

- ≈ 'what's in it for me' to 'what can I give to you'

- ≈ 'look at what I made' to 'look at what we created'.

Just imagine how work could feel if everyone showed up like that. It has to start somewhere. It's going to start with *you*.

A TUBE FULL OF HUMOUR

My friend Jay Martens is an internationally renowned event director and curator. Over the last 20 years he's designed and delivered world-class conferences and events on every continent, and I'm fortunate enough to call him a friend and colleague. When I told him about the premise for this book, and specifically about finding the courage to give, he told me about an experience he had on the tube in London.

> It was peak hour on the Piccadilly line. Middle of winter, bitterly cold and the tube was packed. Despite the close physical proximity we had to one another, everyone on that train were miles apart. Buried deep in a book, or submerged in the infinite scroll of a smart phone. No eye contact, headphones on, you could hear a pin drop throughout the carriage.
>
> Then out of nowhere, the tube driver starts speaking into the intercom: 'Ladies and gentlemen, this is your captain speaking. We're currently cruising

(continued)

A TUBE FULL OF HUMOUR (cont'd)

at an altitude of 1 foot, our flight path looks clear, weather is favourable, so we're hoping to touch down in Kensington just a few seconds ahead of schedule. If you'd like to kick back, make the most of this fair weather and enjoy all the tube has to offer. Once again, thank you for travelling with us.'

As he spoke you could see a few wry smiles starting to appear on the passengers' faces. A few people pulled out their headphones. Some of us even made eye contact.

As we pulled into Kensington station, just like we'd all done a thousand times before, something interesting happened. The train came to a standstill, people moved toward the doors to exit, but the doors didn't open. If you've ever been on the tube, you know this is quite unsettling.

'Good morning once again ladies and gents, this is your captain speaking. We've just landed in beautiful South Kensington and the local weather forecast is for sunshine. But let's be honest, we're in London, so that's highly unlikely.'

By now the entire train were engaged, with more eye contact between passengers and more laughter puncturing the silence.

'You're probably wondering why the doors are still locked,' he continued. 'Well, I thought we could make it interesting this morning. For all of you in a rush, I'm stealing 30 seconds of your day to make you smile. So if you'll join me for a count down from three, I'll open these doors and liberate you from your carriage. Three ... did I tell you about the weather? Oh yes, I did that already ...

Three ... two ... one ... whoops, wrong button. Forgive me, folks. Let's take it from the top one more time ...'

At this point the whole train was alive with laughter. Faces were lit up, we were connecting with each other, pulled out of our Monday morning dread.

'Okay everyone, for the last time ... three ... two ... one ... have a marvellous day, folks!' he shouted. As the doors flew open a sea of revitalised, joyful people fell out of the tube. We bounced our way through a wall of bewildered commuters standing on the platform. I can only imagine how bizarre we must've looked to the people waiting to walk onto the train.

That simple act of creative kindness gave everyone on that train a moment to remember. A moment we're still talking about almost a decade later.

The tube driver's willingness to give us his personality, to offer his self-expression in the service of strangers, to sacrifice his 'professionalism' to inspire and motivate us to see our world differently, was breathtaking.

This is the magic of giving. The power of what's possible when you offer your self-expression in service of those you work with. To give the gift of you, when it matters most.[43]

---

[43] If you've ever been to Melbourne and were fortunate enough to travel on the number 48 tram, you might've experienced the magic of Bruce Whalley. He's been dubbed Melbourne's happiest tram driver and is known for the hilarious commentary he provides his passengers as the tram snakes it's way through the streets of Melbourne (like singing Christmas carols or having a laugh with bicycle riders).

Look for the *not* obvious

As Jay's story shows us, giving isn't just about sharing ideas; it's about sharing yourself. About finding the courage to contribute whatever you can, whenever you can, however you can. It's about presence and joy, and surprise and delight. There are an infinite number of ways you can give in the workplace and here are a few not-so-obvious yet highly impactful things you can give to the people around you:

≈ **Recognition.** We've all heard the adage, 'people don't quit their job, they quit their boss', and according to research by The O.C. Tanner Institute, up to 79 per cent of employees cite a lack of acknowledgement as a reason for leaving. In the current landscape, almost everyone feels undervalued and underappreciated. Why not give a little more love? Let them know you see them and value them. Look for ways to hero or highlight the creative efforts of others. Honour and celebrate the courage it takes for anyone to be creative in their work and life.

≈ **Attention.** We are living in such a shallow, transient age. Where your number of Instagram followers determines your worth. Everyone is half in the moment, half considering their next move, assessing whether you're worth the time. So commit to being fully present with whoever you're with. No looking over shoulders at networking events, no looking at your phone during meetings. Give your full focus and attention to whoever stands before you. And watch the sheer delight in your colleagues as they *finally* feel seen, heard, acknowledged and appreciated.

≈ **Secrets.** Life is too short to keep secrets. Why not give away all the ways you figured out how to kick arse at work? All the hacks and tricks you've discovered through trial and error? Share them. Make life easier for the people around you. Whether it's a cheap carpark, or a great coffee shop, or a few shortcuts on the laptop, help the people around you rise with you. And inevitably, they'll start sharing all their secrets with you.

≈ **Connections.** Always be on the lookout for how someone you just met might be of value to someone you already know (and

160

vice versa). The exponential impact you can have by connecting two people that are perfect for each other is astonishing. And the unintended benefit is that if they go on to build a meaningful, long-term relationship, they will always equate their collective success with you!

≈ **Empowerment.** When I first met my buddy Phil, he said, 'Myke, I'm in. I believe in what you're doing. From now on, whenever you say jump, I'll say how high!' I can't tell you what a difference it makes, knowing that someone has your back. That they'd go into battle for you, support your every decision and stand up for you when you're not around. Be your version of Phil to your colleagues. Champion them, advocate for them, empower them to be the best version of themselves. Be the best friend, confidant, sidekick, number 1 fan, Sam from *Lord of the Rings* kind of colleague that everyone wishes they had.

Constantly ask 'How can I make their work, their life, this moment better for them in some way?'

Humble yourself with gratitude

As a final thought for this chapter, and to bring this virtuous circle of creativity to a close, it's helpful to remember just how big the world is and just how small we really are.

Right now, there are 7.5 billion people on the planet, and it's estimated approximately 108 billion have come and gone throughout history. All of whom have had ideas about life, love, work and the universe. The probability of you coming up with anything original or anything on your own is pretty much…zero.

You don't exist in a vacuum. You're a product of your genes, your environment, your influences. All of which were given to you.

Your life is an ongoing conversation with the world around you. A selfless exchange that asks nothing in return. And at some point, it's important to stop, exhale and appreciate the magnitude of your existence.

It is a miracle you were even born. The astonishing sequence of serendipity that took place for your parents to meet, and their parents to meet. And on and on and on until the dawn of our species.

The infinite dance of choice and chance that had to happen for you to be who you are and where you are is beyond comprehension. You are the product of the universe's creative process. A gift from the world, to the world, just as the world is a gift to you.

'Whoa there, tiger! I thought this was a book about creativity and making magic at work! We're getting a bit deep now, aren't we?'

Yeah we are! And it's about time. If we allowed ourselves to get present to how extraordinarily fortunate we are, it's impossible not to be floored with feelings of gratitude. To recognise that generosity and abundance are fundamental to life itself.

The only way we can ever repay life for everything it's given to us is to follow its lead. To surrender ourselves in service of something greater than ourselves. To join the constellation of human stars that already shine so that others may find their way. Back to themselves, back to creativity, back to gratitude.

If you allow this idea to penetrate your heart, your work takes on a whole new meaning. You'll begin to realise your success is not defined by what you make, but by what you give away. You'll see that the outcomes of your creative practice were never intended for you, they were always meant for the world.

You'll come to accept that you are merely an instrument. A conduit. A temporary production haus for the divine to express itself through you. Your reward is not the recognition or remuneration you may receive. Your reward is that you get to seek, feel, make and give. Your reward is that you get to express your gratitude by being as generous with the world as it's been with you.

Every. Single. Day.

TIME TO PLAY

Choose one of these to action this week.

≈ **Launch an #AMA.** Put a daily (or weekly) block in your calendar and invite your colleagues to join you for an 'Ask Me Anything' session. Tell them you're available to answer any questions they have within whatever parameters you determine. It could be about your career or the future of the company. You could be asked for advice or asked just to listen. It could be about technical knowledge or philosophical ideas. But you're open and ready to give presence, expertise and experience in service of your team.

≈ **A random act of creativity.** Do something surprising, thoughtful and generous for someone on your team. Or your whole team. Bonus points for doing it for a customer or a stranger. Give them an idea, an experience or a moment that changes the way they see and feel about the world. Just like the tube driver in London (or Bruce Whalley in Melbourne).

≈ **Give away your best ideas.** James Altucher, the author and investor, thinks up then shares 10 new ideas every day. He doesn't have the time to do them all, but he thinks someone in the world might. So rather than letting them go to waste on a hard drive, he shares them without asking for credit or compensation.

≈ **Make a connection.** Connect two people in a creative way that you believe will add value to each other. Be sure to set each person up for success by being thoughtful in the way you introduce them/describe them. Bonus points for connecting people that cut you out of the equation but make their lives and work better.

≈ **Invite others to give.** Look for opportunities to give others the opportunity to give. Set up a secret society like Etsy's 'Ministry for Unusual Business' that acknowledges the brilliant yet often unseen work of others. Or start a potluck lunch ritual in the office. Create circumstances that ask the people around you to contribute more of themselves in service of others.

By now you should have...

A deep understanding of the virtuous circle of everyday creativity. And a big bag full of exercises and examples you can apply in your work.

It begins by finding the courage to *seek*.

Developing a healthy distaste for the default. Becoming furiously curious about everything. Learning to ask bigger, broader and more beautiful questions.

This is enhanced by finding the courage to *feel*.

By activating your aesthetic intelligence. Listening for and leveraging your sensory awareness. Being fully present to your surroundings, trusting your authentic feelings and emotions, then synthesising them into something meaningful.

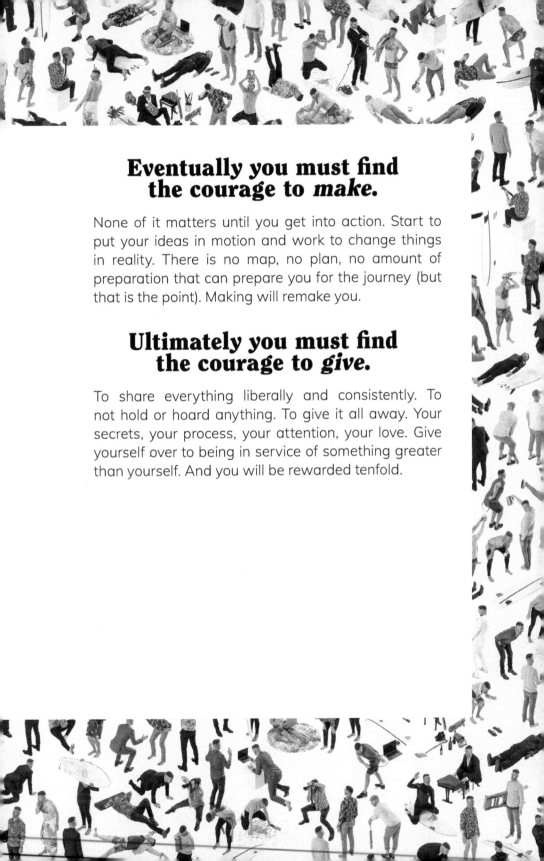

Eventually you must find the courage to *make*.

None of it matters until you get into action. Start to put your ideas in motion and work to change things in reality. There is no map, no plan, no amount of preparation that can prepare you for the journey (but that is the point). Making will remake you.

Ultimately you must find the courage to *give*.

To share everything liberally and consistently. To not hold or hoard anything. To give it all away. Your secrets, your process, your attention, your love. Give yourself over to being in service of something greater than yourself. And you will be rewarded tenfold.

PART THREE

Making Your Masterpiece

By now you're well on your way to becoming an Everyday Creative. You've reclaimed your creative identity, reimagined what you want from your work, and redefined the unique value you have to bring to it.

You've learned about the virtuous circle of Everyday Creativity, and committed to a daily practice of seeking, feeling, making and giving.

All that's left is to dunk your hand into a can of paint, then swirl it all over the canvas that is your life and career.

There are no maps or blueprints. No guidelines to heed or formulas to follow. I did, however, want to leave you with a few final considerations: ideas that you can use when it suits. Approaches that might make a difference.

It's up to you to make and shape your version of an Everyday Creative. Your only limitation is your imagination.

CHAPTER EIGHT
Little Things

...often make
the biggest difference.

There's an overused African proverb, 'If you want to go fast, go alone. If you want to go far, go together.' When it comes to sustaining everyday creativity in your work, bringing your colleagues on the journey with you isn't just preferable, it's powerful!

In this chapter, you're going to learn five secret weapons to influence the people you work with to lean a little further into their everyday creativity.

Five flavour enhancers
for the fabulous

Think of these five elements as an expanded colour palette that you can use to make your work more vivid and vibrant. To draw people into your ideas or empower them to step forward into their own.

They're like the cucumber in your G&T, the truffle shavings on your scrambled eggs, the dark chocolate in your bolognese sauce.[44] They'll

---

[44] Do you doubt me? Try it. I dare you. It's a game changer. And if you have any revolutionary recipe tips for me, I'm all ears — mykel@mykeldixon.com.

help you make the promise of becoming a creative company or team way more appealing and way more delicious.

#1: Optimism

When you consider how much the media bombards us with messages of doom and gloom, is it any wonder most people err on the side of pessimism? To think all these narratives aren't influencing the way we are at work isn't just naive — it's deluded.

But here's the thing: we don't need another 'realist' in the workplace. 'Realism' is usually just a mask for fear, laziness or cynicism. We need *optimistic* realists: people who see the world as it is but choose to work proactively and progressively toward what it could be.

It's far too easy to complain, find fault or make a case for why something cannot or will not work. But to stand with two feet in hope is to walk against the tide of our time.

Far from being flaky or airy-fairy, remaining positive in the face of negativity, criticism and doubt requires profound discipline.

No matter what the odds, and despite the data, an Everyday Creative stays centred in the possibility of *anything*. They summon the courage and creativity to relentlessly put forward new ideas, alternative options or fresh perspectives.

I'm not saying you need to be rainbow bubblegum all day, every day. Lord knows I need a good whinge every now and then, especially when I'm faced with an insidious injustice or infuriating incompetence. But you've got to develop a strategy for shaking it off and getting back to the glass half full.

Who would you rather work with? Someone who can always find fault, or someone who always looks for fortune? Someone who complains about the rain, or someone who invites you dance in it?

Here are three quick hacks that work for me when I start losing my optimism:

1. **Write and delete.** Whenever I've been shot or shut down for being different or speaking out, I schedule a quiet moment

alone, then write all my frustrations down. Sometimes as a letter to the person who attacked me. Sometimes as a journal entry. I get it all out, I read it through, rewrite it if I need to, then I delete it. There's no need to keep it and certainly no need to send it. Getting it out of my head through my hands is almost as cathartic as deleting it from my hard drive.

2. **Walk it off.** The brain is a beautiful thing but it can get stuck in a dangerous loop. The simplest way I've found to shake off a shitty circumstance is to go for a good ol' walk. To move this glorious bag of bones I've been given. If you're at work, just politely excuse yourself and head outside. Get the endorphins flowing, let the air cleanse the palate of your mind.

3. **Get back to gratitude.** It's pretty hard to feel hard done by when you're standing in gratitude. If I'm stuck in a circle of cynicism, I'll often make a quick gratitude list. Writing out everyone and everything that has made my life possible until this point is a powerful way to re-centre myself. Use a napkin, or the back of an electricity bill, or the Notes app in your smart phone. Take two minutes, tops. Don't think, just write. What had to happen today, yesterday, last year or decade for you to be here? (Side note — it doesn't work to just re-read an old list; the magic is in writing it. Watch the words fall out of your pen.)

#2: Tenacity

I hate to break it to you, but when you set off to make your work a work of art, a lot of people won't understand, acknowledge or appreciate what you're trying to do. If your quest involves them in any way, some will seek to avoid you, and some will openly resist. Others will even attempt to sabotage your efforts.

To walk this path requires an unparalleled tenacity in the face of apathy and dissent. The bigger the company, the slower it moves. The more creative the project, the more terrifying the prospect.

To be an Everyday Creative, you've got to have a borderline obsession for getting things done, a natural addiction for finding work-arounds and a congenital incapacity to even hear the words, 'That'll never work'.

Creative work is more like a marathon than a sprint. You've got to be in it for the long haul if you're going to find success. It's your grit that gives you an edge.

What's important to recognise, however, is that it's not the hard approach that wins, nor the size of your desire; it's merely your persistence. The relentless resilience to show up and be creative, day in, day out, year after year.

And in the same way a steady flow of water shapes the hardest stone, you will shape the culture of your company.

Great ideas, projects and cultures are not built overnight. This work is rarely wrapped in a neat, convenient box. To borrow a turn of phrase from the reality show *Survivor*, you will 'outwit, outplay and outlast' the people or systems that seek to suppress your self-expression.

Here are three things that work for me when I start losing my grit:

1. **Just do the minimum.** On the days I don't have the juice to bring 100 per cent to the mission, I'll do the bare minimum. Maybe that's writing a single line. Maybe that's managing a single smile. Maybe it's adjusting the font size. No matter how small, or seemingly insignificant, these tiny acts of defiance remind me that I've got what it takes to see it through.

2. **Go back to the beginning.** If you find yourself losing your grip, or wanting to give up, return to your successes. Go back to past wins to remind you who you are and what you're capable of. I have a friend who keeps all the thank you cards and letters they've ever received and when they feel a little beaten down, they pull them out to get present to the good work they've already done. For me, I listen to my old songs. The music that I made, that made me come alive. Those songs might not have topped the charts or made me a million bucks, but they've been

priceless for the way they make me feel when I'm starting to question my capacity to continue.

3. **Pause for power.** Remember, you're not a machine. Every breath is made of an inhale and an exhale. If you're going to sustain your creative aspirations at work, it's vital you give yourself what you need when you need it. And a big part of this is patience: having the fortitude to delay gratification. Having the wisdom to wait. When a project is stopped or scrapped, use the time to regroup, reassess and recharge, then come back stronger than ever.

#3: Humour

We love a joke at home. We love goofing around with our friends and sharing a laugh with strangers. But sadly, we keep a lot of that frivolity out of the office. Somewhere along the line we all subscribed to the idea that professionalism equates to stoicism and earnestness. That if we're to be taken seriously, we should remain serious.

But as Michael Kerr, author of *The Humor Advantage*, points out, 'people who take themselves overly seriously are often, ironically, taken less seriously by the people around them'.

And it's not that we don't see the value of humour in the workplace. In a study conducted by management consulting company Robert Half International, they found 91 per cent of executives believe a sense of humour is important for career advancement while 84 per cent feel that people with a good sense of humour do a better job.

Humour is grossly undervalued in the workplace.

A well-placed and well-intentioned joke can work wonders. It acts like a valve, releasing pressure. It's a catalyst for inciting intimacy and a precursor to psychological safety. Humour has a way of flattening hierarchies, changing perspectives and uniting enemies.

Which is why humour is so essential to your work as an Everyday Creative. You don't have to be Jerry Seinfeld or Melissa McCarthy, but giving the gift of a giggle every now and then is a secret weapon worth exploring.

Science tells us laughter is good for our brain, it's great for our body and it's fantastic for connecting with our colleagues. What's more, in workplaces where humour is openly shared, the culture tends to encourage people to be themselves, which results in a more positive, productive and innovative workplace.

It's important to remember, however, we are living in the age of offence. Our sense of humour could vary greatly from that of other folks in our team. And jokes can so easily be taken out of context (especially when they're directed at someone else).

The key is always intention. An Everyday Creative uses humour to bring joy, illuminate an alternative perspective, or build intimacy within a team. Never to hurt or harm. The humour used by you has got to be heartfelt. Warm and fuzzy. Light and loose. More about giggling than sniggering. More about connecting that isolating. Everyday Creatives laugh *with*, not at.

Here are a few quick ways to play with humour in the workplace:

1. **Be the butt.** The safest way to get a laugh at work is to make fun of yourself. Once, when attempting to make cookies in a workplace, I almost burned the building down by leaving the oven on. Most people saw it as hilarious but a few were less than impressed. So I made a sign with my picture and the words, 'If you see this man, do not let him near the oven'.[45] Self-deprecating humour is a powerful tool for building relationships and lightening the mood. When you're willing to get at laugh at your own expense, you're telling people they can be safe around you. That you're aware of your own faults and eccentricities and that it's okay if they want to reveal their own.

---

[45] You can see a photo of this silliness in the VIP section of the online portal www.everydaycreatives.com

2. **Surprise with contrast.** A lot of the magic of comedy is due to surprise or a mismatched expectation. The punchline is not what we were anticipating, which is why we find it so hilarious. You can play with this dynamic in all sorts of easy, inoffensive ways. Like wrapping a tiny gift in a ridiculously oversized box. Or naming your next project the polar opposite of what you're trying to achieve. Whenever I have a conference call with a new client but the video component isn't working for whatever reason, I'll quickly email a photo of Brad Pitt with a subject line like, 'just so you recognise me at the event'. You don't have to have them curled over in fits of laughter. Just a cheeky moment of surprise and delight can make a world of difference.

3. **Alley-oop questions.** In case you're not familiar with basketball, an alley-oop is when one player throws the ball toward the backboard and another player (their teammate), catches the ball midair then slam dunks it into the basket. A great way to cultivate inclusive humour is to ask leading questions that inevitably result in a hilarious answer. For example, instead of asking a colleague 'how will we measure the success of this project?', you could ask, 'So how will we measure the misery of this project?' Or if you're struggling to choose what kind of catering for an upcoming event you could ask, 'What food has the highest chance of surviving a trip home in a handbag?' You're setting your colleagues up for a hilarious answer by giving them a comedy-inducing question. One that will hopefully result in a slam-dunk of giggles.

How will we measure
the misery of this
project?

Popcorn consumed
Memes generated
Revolutions started
Balloons popped
Paper hats created

#4: Celebration

A lot of my clients speak about the current crunch of work. The deadlines are getting shorter, the budgets are getting smaller. Everyone is under the pump.

This kind of pace is unsustainable at the best of times, but if you're not careful, months can go by before you stop and recognise the great work being done by the people around you.

A brilliant way to bring a little relief to the daily grind is to instigate a culture of celebration. You don't have to wait until you finish the project or finish another year; you can celebrate something every day. And the more random the better.

You can celebrate when Ruben remembers his Keep Cup. Or when three people in your team are all wearing black jeans and a white shirt. Or when a supplier shows up with an invoice.

You can use celebration as way to reaffirm the kinds of behaviours you want to see. Or to find out what's important to your colleagues and clients. But ultimately, celebration is a pathway to joy. It gives you and your team a reason to pause, get present to someone or something, and recognise its value.

An Everyday Creative is always on the hunt for something to celebrate.

This doesn't mean you need to spend a bunch of money or take a lot of time. It just means you're attuned to the infinite number of ways your workplace rocks. And you are constantly encouraging others to know and own their value.

Here are three simple ways to infuse celebration into the fabric of your culture.

1. **Be like the Ministry.** Online maker marketplace Etsy used to have a shadow organisation working within the company. Its sole prerogative was to surprise and delight its employees

through recognition and reward. Its operations were secret, but all employees were encouraged to call on the Ministry when they felt like someone deserved to be celebrated. By anonymously recognising people for good work through personalised notes and small gifts, they capitalised on the psychological value of surprise and delight. How could you start your own shadow organisation at your company? Pull together a small group of people with the sole purpose of celebrating courage and creativity, surprising folks with thoughtful gifts and meaningful moments that highlight the great work they're doing that often goes unnoticed and unrewarded.

2. **Consider personal milestones.** Most of us, most of the time, are working toward something in our personal lives. Be it saving for a mortgage, taking an online course or trying to shave off a few kilos. Making a conscious effort to find out what your colleagues or clients are up to outside of work is a game changer. When you know what's important to them, or what significant milestones they've got coming up, you've got a beautiful bunch of reasons to surprise and delight them when they achieve something that matters to them. Maybe their daughter was just cast in the lead role in the school play. Maybe it's their thirtieth wedding anniversary. Maybe they finally reached the next level in Fortnite. Celebrating their wins, with their permission, shows them that you see them. That you value them for more than just what they do at work.

3. **Keep it fresh.** A celebration has got to be a celebration, it's not an obligation. So you've got to mix it up once in a while. If your weekly meeting to 'share your wins' feels a bit stale, or the annual award event feels a little too familiar, shake it up. Put the meeting at the start of the week. Book a different venue for the Christmas party. Get together with a few colleagues and bake a birthday cake instead of ordering one online. Or, better yet, ask your team what they think makes a great celebration. What else have they seen or done in previous teams or jobs that worked and they loved? Put some of the responsibility in their hands, giving them more ownership over how they like to celebrate and be celebrated.

#5: Squad

Margaret Mead said, 'Never doubt that a small group of thoughtful, committed citizens can change the world; indeed, it's the only thing that ever has.'

Getting a few of your colleagues interested in your creative aspirations is a good start. Building a rock-solid tribe of creative counterparts who share your vision for a more creative company is even better.

When you're building a vision that few others can see or you're standing for values that few others believe in, it's tough. Having a squad of misfits and mavericks that are just as committed as you is powerful.

There's a reason I take my band or my brother with me to conferences and events. Sure, when I bring my band the experience is bigger and better for my audiences. When I bring my brother (who is a filmmaker), I get to capture each performance on film, which is fantastic for marketing or as a value-add for clients.

But all of that pales in comparison to the value I receive from having someone I trust in the room, on the journey with me.

My brother Dave has seen me perform more than anyone on the planet. He knows exactly what I need to hear both pre and post every performance. He's quick to lend a hand, fix a problem or stand up for me when the moment calls. He's absolutely irreplaceable when it comes to giving me the confidence I need to keep being creative.

Similarly, my buddy Phil calls me almost every day. Just to check in and keep the vibe alive. To share a little about what's going on for him and hear a little about what's going on for me. I can't begin to tell you how valuable that is.

In all honesty, it would be easier logistically and better for me financially if I flew solo. But I don't want to sit at the top of a mountain on my own. If I had the choice between summiting alone or sharing the journey with someone else and not quite making the summit, I'd choose the latter every time.

In this game, having people in your corner who you can call on when the heat gets turned up isn't just a nice-to-have, it's essential.

If you are going to be an Everyday Creative you're going to need a Phil, or a Dave, or both.

So how do you find one?

Simple. First, you've got to be one. Relationships aren't a one-way street. Like everything in life that matters, what you put in is what you get out. If you are going to build a tribe around you (and you must), then you're going to have to be a tribe for someone else.

Who do you currently call on for support? Who already has your back no matter what? Who used to be on speed dial but you kinda let it slip?

Don't beat yourself up about it. We all do it. The madness of modern life gets the better of us at the best of times. But commit to calling them up right now. Find out how they're doing. Listen for ways you can help. Not as a way to get something from them.

Just get interested. Be supportive of what matters to them. Send a whole lot of love consistently and unconditionally to the people you want in your life.

Yes, it takes effort. Yes, it's often inconvenient. But man, is it worth it.

Here are some tips on how to build your sacred squad:

1. **Surrender your agenda.** You can smell it when someone wants something from you. When it feels a bit staged or disingenuous. So can your colleagues. We all have a built-in bullshit detector, so if you really want to build a network of (r)evolutionaries, start by putting aside what you want. Make a private commitment to yourself that you're not going to ask for or expect any ROI on any of your relationships. If that sounds

like too much work, you haven't been paying attention. Give it up. Get over yourself. And start by helping them with what's important to them.

2. **Shoot the shit.** The most meaningful, long-lasting relationships I've ever had were not the result of a solitary, peak experience. They were (and are) based on years of ordinary, in-between moments. Everyday conversations, shared silences, time spent in each other's company in any capacity. It makes a massive difference. There are so many reasons to push back against the rapid pace of the modern workplace. But none are more important than to enable real-world face time with the people you work with. Allowing space for just hanging out, waiting for the bus, or watching the world go by. That's when the deep, vulnerable discussions emerge. Don't be afraid to blow off an afternoon of meetings to have a three-hour brunch with your manager. Don't be afraid to share a ride home from the airport with your client. Don't be afraid to talk about everyday stuff, or sit comfortably in silence, or help pack the goodie-bags for the next conference. Doing ordinary things together leads to an extraordinary togetherness.

3. **Make your own myths.** Culture is defined by a shared set of behaviours and beliefs. The personality of any tribe is revealed through their rituals and artefacts. All of it makes and shapes the identity of the collective. When you're forming your sacred squad, be on the look out for moments that can become meaningful memories. For artefacts that can symbolise who you are and what you stand for. Develop rituals that become the architecture of your culture. Whenever the band and I go on the road, it's inevitable we'll return with a song we've written about something ridiculous that happened along the way. It could be about a missed flight, or an overly enthusiastic concierge, or a mixup with soundcheck times. That song becomes the theme song of that tour. On the way home from the airport, I'll send a voice message to the band singing the latest tour theme song. They'll record their pieces of the track over the next few days in their home studios until it's complete.

No-one will ever see or hear these tunes[46]; they're just for us. But they've become part of the glue that keeps us together. This ridiculous ritual reminds us who we are, and empowers us to keep rocking our unique collective identity.

▲ ▲ ▲

This chapter is about doing more of the things we know we could and *should* be doing. Simple, practical things that would make a massive difference to us and the people around us. It's easy to skim over this stuff. To label these ideas as obvious or unrealistic.

But we both know work would be a whole lot better if we were a little more optimistic. If we were a little more tenacious. If we weren't so afraid to have a laugh, weren't so busy to celebrate our hard work and were a little more willing to spend a little more time just being with each other.

Not as colleagues or clients. Not to solve a problem or meet an agenda. Just as people. As humans. As Everyday Creatives.

---

[46] Actually, we're going to record an album of our 'on the road' songs and release it as a free download in the online portal – www.everydaycreatives.com. Stay tuned by registering through the site. (Disclaimer — there might be a few naughty words in the mix.)

CHAPTER NINE
A Big Thing

When your calling
comes calling

At some point, while you're living and working, seeking and feeling, making, giving and being the fabulous Everyday Creative you were born to be, something might happen.

An unexpected impulse to create something else. A subtle yet pervasive desire to shift your focus onto something big. Something that feels foreign yet familiar. Abstract but alluring.

This is when your calling comes calling.

It might come as a whisper or a bang. It might be cryptic or crystal clear. It might arrive as a startling new insight or re-emerge as a long-forgotten memory. Either way, it's often hard to explain but difficult to ignore.

Perhaps it's writing a book or starting a new business. It might be changing careers or changing countries. It could be hosting a week-long event, building an underground movement or standing up and taking bold action on something you believe in.

But it's as scary as it is seductive. As inspiring as it is inconvenient. As compelling as it is way outside your comfort zone.

What is a calling?

A calling differs from the day-to-day responsibilities of your job. It's not defined by the demands of your boss, or your family, or your clients. And it's not something you can achieve in an afternoon or a few weeks.

Your calling is a major project, career or lifestyle change that is personally meaningful to you and requires sustained effort to complete.

A calling insists that you alter the way you live, and restructure the way you work in order to give yourself over to it.

It might be something you have no prior experience with and no previous desire for. It might require you to start from scratch or learn a bunch of stuff before you can even begin.

Whatever it is, when it comes (and it always comes) you will be asked—will you follow me?

At that point you have two options...

(Get a pen and circle the one you choose.)

No

Yes

What happens if you say no?

A lot of folks will tell you that when your calling comes calling, you must drop everything immediately. You've got to grab it with both hands and follow it with reckless abandon.

Some will say the opposite: that a professional is someone who shows up every day, whether they feel inspired or not. They grind out their creative work or career no matter what.

Contrary to popular advice, I'm here to tell you that if you don't follow your calling, it's not the end of the world. The sky won't fall. You won't lose all your hair. In fact, nothing much will change at all.

You can keep doing what you've been doing, keep living how you've been living. Which, of course, means you'll keep getting what you've been getting.

And maybe that's enough for you. At least for now.

Our lives are full of duties, commitments and relationships. It's not always the right time to follow a calling and sometimes the sacrifice or the fallout is too great to make.

However, no matter how noble or legitimate your reasons might be, there are always implications to your refusal.

A calling is a deep universal impulse that burns to be fulfilled. It is impatient in nature and it won't wait for *you*. It only cares about manifesting itself in the world in some way. So if you're not the one who says yes when it calls, it *will* find someone else.

This is what happens when a few months or years go by and you meet or hear about someone who is doing that very thing that came to you in a dream. Someone else who heeded the call that once came to you.

Don't you just hate it when that happens? It drives me nuts. I get all jealous, angry and bitter. I look for the ways that they're failing. Tell myself I could've and would've done it better. Avoiding at all cost the undisputed truth: that I didn't.

If, however, you did decide to heed the call. If, despite your reservations, you couldn't find a good enough reason to say no … things get a whole lot more interesting.

So what happens if you say yes?

When your calling comes calling and you follow it fully, you set in motion a series of events you cannot imagine.

Coincidences and serendipities. Mystic symbols and cryptic signs. Everything you see and everyone you meet will feel as though they're part of an unfurling story. That they're all pushing you toward this quest, this moment, this choice.[47]

---

[47] My fabulous editor Ali thought this paragraph might be getting a little too esoteric. But I reckon we're all the way in now. Bring on the magic and the mystic, the oblique and the abstract, the arty farty, fluffy puffy madness! I've been holding it for eight chapters!!!

187

It's inevitable that your calling will distract you from your daily work. It'll wake you up in the middle of the night. It'll cause you to question the very foundation of what you thought your life was for.

And sure, this can be unsettling. But it's equally thrilling. And with every step you take toward the fulfilment of your big thing, the world takes a hundred toward you.

How to keep saying yes

In the beginning, when you follow your calling, you might feel a little clumsy or way out of your depth. But this is perfectly natural. To start with you might even be too shy to tell anyone about it, fearful that they'll laugh or warn you of the dangers of such a decision.

≈ 'Write a book?' they'll say, 'But you don't even have a blog!'

≈ 'Start your own business?' they'll say, 'And where will you get the money for that?'

≈ 'Move to the country?' they'll say, 'And throw away your career? But you worked so hard to get where you are. Are you sure that's what you want?'

Most of the time they're just trying to help. Some of the time they're just projecting their own fears and regrets.

And let's be honest, we can sound a little crazy when, entirely out of the blue, we start speaking about a vision, a dream or a calling. Something wild and adventurous that is creative or unconventional. Something that requires us to give up, let go of or set fire to what we've already built.

So how do you reassure the people around you that you're not having a mid-life crisis? How do you find a level of confidence when you have no level of competence? How do you keep going when you have no real idea of where you're even heading?

It's time to trust

yourself.
#justsayin

A calling will re-create you

What we misunderstand about a calling and about building big things is that before you begin you aren't ready, you're not equipped and you never will be. At least not if you keep standing there.

The only way you'll develop the skills necessary to build that big thing is by building that big thing. The only way you become the kind of person who follows that creative calling is by following that creative calling.

You become who you need to become on the journey. Not before and not after. The quest, the outcome and you are all inextricably linked.

And this is the biggest gift of all. You are rebuilt in the process of building your big thing. You are remade in the process of remaking your life. You are reformed in the process of forming the realisation of your dreams.

It's the making that makes you.

So if you've heard the call, found the courage to follow it and you know that you'll never be prepared but that's the point ... what next? What else might help you when you're walking on your way?

I think it's helpful to remember that a calling is three things:

1. seasonal

2. personal

3. universal.

#1: A calling is seasonal

As you're building your big thing, you're going to have wild moments of magic. Bursts of astonishing inspiration. Fits of furious passion and electrifying excitement. Especially in the beginning. But you'll also have moments of doubt, long plateaus and a lack of drive. There will be roadblocks and setbacks. U-turns and detours. Three steps forward and two steps back.

You might even have to put your big thing on hold. For a few days, a few months or even a few years. Unforeseen circumstances or unavoidable emergencies may require your attention for longer than you'd like.

That's all part of the process. There is value in putting down the paintbrush, taking an extended break and filling your days with different ways, or different people, or different places.

When you eventually return you'll have a new perspective on things. New ideas to throw into the mix, new approaches or skills or connections you can use to continue and possibly finish your project.

It's also worth noting that what you end up with—the finished product of your process—might not look or feel anything like what you originally intended. And that's also part of the game. I like to think the vision we were given was just the spark we needed to start the fire. But the fire itself changes shape many times over. Every log we place on it adds to the colour, configuration and heat. Even conditions outside our control, like the wind or rain, can influence the size and shape of the fire.

Again, it's all part of the process.

And, like the seasons we live in, they keep on moving, from one to the next. The bitter cold, the searing heat, the blooming flowers or falling leaves—all temporary, all linked, all beautiful in their own way.

#2: A calling is personal

Another defining characteristic of your calling is that it's yours. Perhaps the essence of the idea could be adopted by anyone, but the way that you embrace it, the way that you build and become it, is unequivocally yours.

Which reiterates the core theme of this book: that your creative process is itself creative and subjective. That the way you build your big thing will be different from how I would build my big thing.

This is your calling. Everyone's will look different. Everyone's will feel different.

Think of your calling like leaving home for the first time. It's moving to the city and getting your first apartment. It's wearing what you want to wear and eating what you want to eat.

It's liberating and terrifying all at once. You can finally do what you want to do, but now you're entirely responsible for yourself. There's no-one else to cook you meals, or pick up your stuff, or take you to your uncle's place for tea.

You have to find your own way there. You have to find your own way everywhere.

It's the final step in fully realising your creative self.

#3: A calling is universal

Finally, every calling is always one small (or large) part of a bigger story: a shared story that involves every one of us. Every species, landscape, ancestor and soon-to-be-soul that is involved in this marvellous thing we call life.

At the core of every calling is an intention to lift, connect and delight the human spirit. To incite more beauty, meaning, mystery and awe; to invoke more reverence for and connection to the divine.

A calling is almost always about love.

About building something that has a positive impact on the planet.

That's not to say everything you create has to be about rainbows and lollipops. Or that the projects you design have to be about saving children or planting trees.

But in essence, it's about being a meaningful contribution to the world. About being a life-affirming force in your family or with your friends. A beacon of hope in your neighbourhood or your workplace. It's about doing magnificent things.

Perhaps your calling asks you to draw cartoons about the unintended impact of divorce. Or highlight the injustices of the political elite. Perhaps your calling asks you to build safer workplaces for women by hosting vulnerability retreats for men. Or maybe your calling asks you to bridge the racial divide in your neighbourhood by building a community garden in your front yard.[48]

All of these things are real life examples of Everyday Creatives who felt compelled to do something else, even if they didn't know how to do it, didn't know what it would take, didn't know where to start.

But they did start and the world is better off because of it.

If you're lucky to ever come face to face with your calling, I hope you take it. For all our sakes. Sure, it won't be easy, it probably won't make sense, but the best things never do.

---

[48] Check out illustrator Gavin Aung Than, who launched Zen Pencils in 2012, a cartoon blog that adapts inspirational quotes into comic stories. Or Anand Giridharadas, who worked as a consultant for McKinsey before quitting to become a journalist/author and later publishing *Winner Take All: The Elite Charade of Changing the World*, which presented an eye-opening attack on the 1 per cent (including McKinsey). As well as the team at Tomorrow Man, an Aussie collective reinventing masculinity in the twenty-first century. Or Ron Finley, the guerilla gardener who has transformed his inner-city community by teaching people how to grow their own food.

A Final Thing

As we're almost about to go our separate ways,[48] I guess it's time I levelled with you: I wasn't entirely honest when we set out on our journey together.

Yes, I want you to do well at work. I want you to come up with brilliant ideas and build radical things. I want you to create beautiful experiences for your clients and enjoy meaningful relationships with your colleagues. And I absolutely want you to find more success and fulfilment in your career and life, and become an Everyday Creative.

But I want something else.

I want you to recognise that unleashing your creative potential is bigger than your career. It's bigger than selling a few thousand books, or lifting your engagement scores a few decimal points. It's bigger than you.

The world needs your creativity. Now more than ever. We need all hands on deck to tackle some of the biggest challenges of our time. We need you to find and follow your joy, curiosity and passion so that you begin (or continue) to dream, design and deliver things that matter. Things that make our world better.

---

[48] Noooooooooooo! This can't be the end! I can't bear it. Head over to the online portal so we can stay connected forever!

195

Sure, we need large scale reform, we need big corporations to change their practices, we need a global shift in mindset and behaviour. But we also need more fully engaged, courageous, open-hearted people who are willing to speak out and stand for more meaningful workplaces.

And it starts by reclaiming your identity. By reimagining the possibility of your work and redefining your unique value.

It's amplified by developing a daily practice of seeking, feeling, making and giving. By rekindling a sense of wonder, activating your aesthetic intelligence, developing a bias for action and embracing a spirit of generosity.

And it is absolutely enhanced by optimism, tenacity, humour, celebration and sense of community.

But all of that is just so that you're in a better position to hear and heed your calling.

Your calling, all callings—your big thing and all big things—are about getting this planet back on track. About building a world that works for all of us.

The most important creative work of your life is to create your life.

To consciously design your mindset, behaviour, relationships and environment. To shape the way you show up in service of others. To make each and every moment a vivid, vibrant expression of your infinite human potential.

Now is the time to make your work a work of art. To make your life a living song that lingers long after you're gone. To inspire others to seek, find and build their own instruments, reclaim their voice and sing.

This is not the end; it's just the beginning. And I can't wait to see what kind of magic you create.

Big love

Where To From Here?

If you haven't already, head over to the online portal, **www.everydaycreatives.com,** use the code **IAMCREATIVE** and register to get lifetime access to the resources I've made for you.

You'll find a plethora of videos, interviews and downloadable worksheets that expand on the concepts in this book, as well as deep-dives into other delightfully dangerous territory.

If you'd love to work with me directly, I speak regularly at conferences and events all over the world, as well as helping leaders and teams design programs and interventions that unleash the full creative potential of their people.

And if you just feel like reaching out, nothing makes me happier than connecting with other Everyday Creatives. So pah-lease don't be shy. Hit me up at: mykel@mykeldixon.com

Let's make a little magic *together!*

I dare you!

www.mykeldixon.com
www.everydaycreatives.com
mykel@mykeldixon.com

Gratitude

Ahhh. Gratitude. The best bit. Can I speak openly for a moment ... writing a book is f@#king hard. Who'd a thunk it. It's a glorious, heart-breaking, terrifying, exhilarating, I'm-never-doing-it-again, best-moment-of-your-life adventure. And there is no way I could've written this one without the help of a phenomenal cast of everyday creatives.

Firstly, to my fabulous editor Kelly Irving, this book would not have happened if it weren't for you. Thank you for sticking with me, for embracing my edits of your edits, and for learning to speak a little of my love language. You are an extraordinary talent and anyone considering writing a book needs to speak to you.

To my second fabulous editor, Allison Hiew, it's almost illegal how delightful you are. The gentle, generous way you suggested ideas and reconfigured sentences didn't just make my writing better. You made me feel like I should start saying 'author' when a customs officer asks me what I do.

To the magnificent Lucy Raymond for not only green lighting this project, but for continually reminding me—and anyone within earshot—that this book matters. That even in the middle of a global pandemic, especially in the middle of a global pandemic, we need to get it out there. Sheesh ... Empowering much?

To the magnanimous Chris Shorten, what a Zen-like Artisan you are. Always available to bounce ideas, or pivot the direction. Quite possibly the most patient man in the entire universe. And I should know. I blew out every single deadline you gave me.

To the outrageous talent that is, Oli Sansom. You beautiful bastard. When a cover concept becomes the basis of an entire brand you know you're onto something. Your talent and tenacity, spirit and selflessness, creativity and charisma knows no bounds. I am so grateful, inspired and moved by you, by our friendship and by your ongoing contribution to my career.

To my Ronin-from-another-mother, Jason Fox. My life would look profoundly different had I not met you. As always, you have been instrumental at every stage of this process. It's a daily thrill to walk a few moons behind you, using your footsteps to guide, inspire or save me on my journey.

To the astonishing Josie Gibson, for seeing and celebrating the mongrel in me. Your unwavering advocacy is unparalleled and my life (and this book) is richer and more meaningful having you in it.

To my bro Dave and beautiful band, Phil, Danny, Trig and Marcel, you guys are the best. I love every single moment we share and create together—on and off stage. I can't wait to bring the ideas in this book to life in front of audiences and organisations around the world.

To all the folks who featured in this book, Laura, Aimee, Shane, Jay, Daz, Gary. To the beautiful souls who helped with my research, Ben, Dean, Eglantine, Dom, Jane, Mikey, the list goes on. And to all my clients and colleagues who inspired so much of the writing...THANK YOU!

To my boys, Sonny Phoenix and Dusty Roc. Without a doubt, you're both the best thing I've ever created. You don't need this book yet and I get the feeling you never will. #naturalborncreatives

But most of all, the biggest slice of love and gratitude goes to my darling Kate. Thank you for your unwavering support through the entire process. You worked twice as hard as I did to get this book done.

Taking care of the boys (all three of them). Making sure I was eating and sleeping and staying on track. Listening patiently as I reworked ideas, unleashed my frustrations, or hatched detailed plans to quit writing and skip town. You are the bees knees, the ducks nuts, and my BFF for realz.

And lastly, thank you to you, dear reader. Nothing is more precious than the gift of your attention. I truly hope this book unlocks something for you and delivers just what you need to start, continue or finish the work that most makes you feel alive.

Buckets of love and light to us all.

Sources

Chapter 1

Fredrick Winslow Taylor and The Principles of Scientific Management— https://en.wikipedia.org/wiki/Scientific_management

The Committee of Ten—https://en.wikipedia.org/wiki/Committee_of_ Ten

'Do Schools Kill Creativity?' TED talk, Ken Robinson—https://www .ted.com/talks/sir_ken_robinson_do_schools_kill_creativity?language=en

The Element: How finding your passion changes everything—Ken Robinson, Penguin Random House, 2009.

UNICEF ranks Australian Schools 39 out of 41—https://www. educationmattersmag.com.au/unicef-report-card-ranks-australia-3941- in-education/ & https://www.smh.com.au/cqstatic/gwsaer/unicef.JPG

Seth Godin quote from *The Icarus Deception: How high will you fly?*, Penguin Group USA, 2012.

Chapter 2

Gallup disengagement study—https://www.gallup.com/workplace/ 238079/state-global-workplace-2017.aspx

Australian loneliness report — https://psychweek.org.au/wp-content/uploads/2018/11/Psychology-Week-2018-Australian-Loneliness-Report.pdf; https://researchbank.swinburne.edu.au/items/c1d9cd16-ddbe-417f-bbc4-3d499e95bdec/1/

World Economic Forum and loneliness — https://www.weforum.org/agenda/2019/08/the-millennial-friendship-crisis/

UK Minister for Loneliness — https://www.nytimes.com/2018/01/17/world/europe/uk-britain-loneliness.html

Australian Call for Minster of Loneliness — https://www.theguardian.com/society/2018/oct/19/loneliness-minister-proposed-to-tackle-australian-social-isolation

Diverse and inclusive workplace more proactive and innovative — https://www.forbes.com/sites/annapowers/2018/06/27/a-study-finds-that-diverse-companies-produce-19-more-revenue/#56f6e7f1506f; https://www.mybusiness.com.au/human-resources/868-study-finds-diverse-inclusive-workplaces-more-productive; https://www.weforum.org/agenda/2019/04/business-case-for-diversity-in-the-workplace/; https://elearningindustry.com/socializing-workplace-important-team-productivity

IBM Study on CEO and creativity — https://www-03.ibm.com/press/us/en/pressrelease/31670.wss

World Economic Forum Future Skills Report on creativity — http://www3.weforum.org/docs/WEF_Future_of_Jobs_2018.pdf

LinkedIn skills companies need (creativity) — https://learning.linkedin.com/blog/top-skills/the-skills-companies-need-most-in-2019–and-how-to-learn-them

Adobe — State of Create, https://www.adobe.com/content/dam/acom/en/max/pdfs/AdobeStateofCreate_2016_Report_Final.pdf

McKinsey Creativity Index — https://www.mckinsey.com/business-functions/mckinsey-digital/our-insights/creativitys-bottom-line-how-winning-companies-turn-creativity-into-business-value-and-growth

Foundation For Young Australians — http://www.fya.org.au/wp-content/uploads/2015/08/fya-future-of-work-report-final-lr.pdf

NESTA research—https://www.nesta.org.uk/report/creativity-vs-robots/

Automation Readiness Paper—https://automationreadiness.eiu.com/ whitepaper

CSIRO—https://data61.csiro.au/en/Our-Research/Our-Work/Future-Cities/Planning-sustainable-infrastructure/Tomorrows-Digitally-Enabled-Workforce

UNICEF ranks Australian School 39 out of 41—https://www.educationmattersmag.com.au/unicef-report-card-ranks-australia-3941-in-education/ & https://www.smh.com.au/cqstatic/gwsaer/unicef.JPG

Gavin Nascimento, founder of a NewKindOfHuman .com—https://anewkindofhuman.com/creative-genius-divergent-thinking-test/

Chapter 3

Simply Brilliant—William C. Taylor, Portfolio, 2016, https://www.goodreads.com/book/show/29093324-simply-brilliant

Eating the Big Fish—Adam Morgan, Wiley, 2009, https://www.goodreads.com/book/show/129985.Eating_the_Big_Fish?ac=1&from_search=true&qid=aqAEc5x1v3&rank=1

Chapter 4

Michael Housman from Cornerstone—https://www.economist.com/the-economist-explains/2013/04/10/how-might-your-choice-of-browser-affect-your-job-prospects

The Seeking System—research by Panksepp https://www.researchgate.net/publication/; 231520837_Panksepp's_SEEKING_System_Concepts_and_Their_Implications_for_the_Treatment_of_Depression_with_Deep-Brain_Stimulation

Martin Seligman on zest—https://en.wikipedia.org/wiki/Zest_(positive_psychology)

Curious—Ian Leslie, Basic Books, 2015, https://www.goodreads.com/book/show/22047408-curious

'Why Curiosity Matters', Francesca Gino—https://hbr.org/2018/09/curiosity

Survey Monkey Study on curiosity—https://hbr.org/2018/09/research-83-of-executives-say-they-encourage-curiosity-just-52-of-employees-agree

Mihaly Csikszentmihaly on creativity—https://www.goodreads.com/en/book/show/40389418

Jonah Leher, 'The virtures of daydreaming'—https://www.newyorker.com/tech/frontal-cortex/the-virtues-of-daydreaming

George Carlin and Vuja De—https://hbr.org/2008/06/what-george-carlin-taught-inno

Chapter 5
The Castle (the movie)—https://en.wikipedia.org/wiki/The_Castle_(1997_Australian_film)

95% of decisions subconscious—https://hbswk.hbs.edu/item/the-subconscious-mind-of-the-consumer-and-how-to-reach-it

The experience economy—https://hbr.org/1998/07/welcome-to-the-experience-economy

Expedia Study on experience—https://www.luxurytraveladvisor.com/running-your-business/stats-74-percent-americans-prioritize-experiences-over-products

Investing in experiences—https://www.under30experiences.com/blog/the-science-of-travel-happiness

Secret Cinema—https://www.secretcinema.org/

Black Tomato and Get Lost—https://www.blacktomato.com/get-lost/

Aesthetic Intelligence—Pauline Brown, Harper Business, 2019, https://www.harpercollins.com/9780062883308/aesthetic-intelligence/

Anticipation of experience—https://journals.sagepub.com/doi/abs/10.1177/0956797614546556

Peak End Rule—https://en.wikipedia.org/wiki/Peak%E2%80%93end_rule

Finite and Infinite Games—James Carse, Free Press, 2013, https://www.goodreads.com/book/show/189989.Finite_and_Infinite_Games

Chapter 6
Atomic Habits—James Clear, Penguin, 2018, https://www.goodreads.com/book/show/40121378-atomic-habits?ac=1&from_search=true&qid=H4Lwi9sdzy&rank=1

Herbie Hancock on Miles Davis—https://www.youtube.com/watch?v=FL4LxrN-iyw

Chapter 7
Research by The Greater Good Science Center for The Templeton Foundation, https://ggsc.berkeley.edu/images/uploads/GGSC-JTF_White_Paper-Generosity-FINAL.pdf

Elizabeth Gilbert on TED—https://www.ted.com/talks/elizabeth_gilbert_your_elusive_creative_genius

Brian Eno on scenius—https://www.wired.com/2008/06/scenius-or-comm/

Austin Kleon on scenius—https://austinkleon.com/2017/05/12/scenius/

Susan Credle—www.nytimes.com/2012/02/26/business/susan-credle-of-leo-burnett-usa-on-sharing-ideas-at-work.html?pagewanted=all

Ursula Franklin quote—https://www.youtube.com/watch?v=7UJkrZ396VI

Research by The O.C. Tanner Institute – https://www.octanner.com/insights/white-papers.html

Chapter 8
Robert Half International study on humour in workplace—https://www.roberthalf.com/blog/accounting-and-finance-blog#xd_co_f=YmQ5NDQ5ZWMtOTM2ZS00Njc3LWJlMWMtODNlZjM2YjU3NGI3~

Laughing with colleagues—https://www.springerprofessional.de/en/when-sharing-a-laugh-means-sharing-more-testing-the-role-of-shar/11733488

The Humor Advantage—Michael Kerr, Humor at Work, 2015, https://www.goodreads.com/book/show/25508630-the-humor-advantage

Index